NATURE RESERVES mentioned in text

1	Askaniya-Nova	**9**	Kronotsky
2	Barguzin	**10**	Lazovsky
3	Barsa Kelmes	**11**	North Ossetia
4	Caucasus	**12**	Pechora-Ilych
5	Central Siberian	**13**	Sikhote Alin
6	Ilmen	**14**	Teberda
7	Kabardino-Bakarsky	**15**	Ust-Lensky
8	Kandalaksha	**16**	Wrangel Island

ARCTIC OCEAN

WRANGEL ISLAND

■ 16

BERING SEA

CHU

TAIMYR PENINSULA

• Norilsk

SIBERIA

Lena

KAMCHATKA PENINSULA

■ 9

SEA OF OKHOTSK

SAKHALIN

KURIL ISLANDS

Angara

LAKE BAIKAL

■ 2

Irkutsk

Amur

Khabarovsk

SIKHOTE ALIN

Ussuri

LAKE KHANKA

■ 13

■ 10

Vladivostok

SEA OF JAPAN

THE NATURE OF
RUSSIA

AUTHOR'S NOTE

At the time of writing, the Soviet Union is in a state of transformation. 'Soviet Union' and 'USSR' are now outdated terms but as there are no replacements as yet, their usage is inevitable. References in this book to 'the world's largest country', meaning the USSR, remain valid even if applied only to the sheer size of Russia itself (that is, the Russian Republic or Federation).

THE NATURE OF
RUSSIA

JOHN MASSEY STEWART

CROSS RIVER PRESS
A Division of Abbeville Publishing Group
New York

This book is dedicated to all living things in the world's largest country

The extracts from *Vasili and Vasilissa: Siberian Stories* (1981), compiled by N. Kupreyanova, and *Nature Reserves in the USSR* (1989), by M. Davydova and V. Kozhevoi, are reproduced with the kind permission of Progress Publishers, Moscow.

First published in the United States of America in 1992 by Cross River Press, a division of Abbeville Publishing Group, 488 Madison Avenue, New York, NY 10022.

First published in the United Kingdom in 1991 by Boxtree Limited, 36 Tavistock Street, London, WC2E 7PB

Printed and bound by Dai Nippon Printing Co. Ltd., Hong Kong

ISBN 1-55859-470-1

Designed by Sarah Hall
Jacket design by David Goodman
Map by Raymond Turvey

CONTENTS

FOREWORD

Occupying an area of more than 22 million sq km (18 percent of earth's dry land) plus 10 million sq km of a marine economic zone, the ecosystems of my country represent the most important constituent part of our planet's biosphere.

Its boreal forests play an immensely important role in the maintenance of the oxygen balance of our planet. More than 70 percent of the sensitive tundra ecosystem exists in my country. The most productive soils of all – the chernozems or black earth – lie across the steppe zone which, sadly, is now almost ruined by bad agricultural practices. The world's most northerly deserts are found in Soviet Central Asia. Our famous Lake Baikal contains 20 percent of the world's total freshwater supplies; the remarkable purity of its water is the result of its unique but fragile ecosystem which includes about 2100 species of which 700 are found nowhere else on earth.

Alas, today the Soviet Union is better known not as a country of unique landscapes and diverse fauna and flora, but as a country suffering from the major ecological catastrophes of Chernobyl and the Aral Sea. For decades we kept silent about our serious ecological problems and spoke only of our undoubted successes in nature conservation (for instance, the return of the sable, saiga antelope, beaver and European bison from the brink of extinction). But in recent years we have changed this rosy-coloured picture for a black one and now we write only about the destruction of nature in the USSR.

The truth, however, is more complex. About 25 percent of the USSR's territory is permanently polluted and about 30 percent suffers periodically from the long-range transport of pollutants. However, about 45 percent of the territory of the country is still practically virgin nature. This represents 8 percent of the world's dry land (larger, indeed, than Amazonia), and its conservation must become the concern not only of the USSR's scientists but of the entire world community.

In this book John Massey Stewart rightly pays attention to the unique system of 170 nature reserves in the USSR which covers 1.2 percent of the entire country.

I have read this book with much interest. It is a brilliant introduction to the nature of an enormous country still little known in the West. John Massey Stewart has produced a good, objective picture of our ecological problems. But he has also succeeded in showing that, in the words of the popular Russian song, 'not all is sold, not all is lost' in my country.

I am certain of the success of this book and hope that it will help towards a better understanding of the ecological problems of our country and the role it plays in the biosphere.

Professor Nikolay N. Vorontsov
Former USSR Minister of the Environment
Member of Parliament of the Russian Federation
Vice-President, Russian Academy of Natural Sciences
26 November, 1991

ACKNOWLEDGEMENTS

Firstly, I am extremely grateful to Professor N. N. Vorontsov for writing the foreword to this book. Secondly, I wish particularly to thank Steve Howard, Paddy Rawlinson, Victoria Bentata, Sam Sherman and, above all, Gwyneth Learner for their research and substantial help in the preparation of this book.

I would also like to thank Baiba Klintze for her additional research, and Igor Altschuler, environmentalist, Ardalyon Vinokurov, ornithologist, and Leslie Symons, geographer, for kindly reading the text and advising on changes; also Sergei Gorshkov, geographer and environmentalist, for doing the same and for much useful information beforehand. Any unwitting mistakes, of course, are my responsibility.

My grateful thanks are also due to: Terence Armstrong and Isabella Warren of the Scott Polar Research Institute, Cambridge; John Appleby for his information, both published and unpublished, on Russian folk medicine; Tony French, geographer, for his expert help on Chapter 6; David Bell for his information on the Ussuri forest and for vetting Chapter 8; Jackie Johnson and Hugh Jenkins of the Centre for Russian and East European Studies, University of Birmingham; Zbigniew Karpowicz of IUCN, and Chris Magin and Graham Drucker of the invaluable World Conservation Monitoring Centre (IUCN, UNED and WWF joint-venture); Gina Douglas, librarian of the Linnean Society; Helen O'Connor, librarian of the Great Britain–USSR Association; David Prynn for information on the animals of the Soviet Far East; Anthony Sutcliffe and Andrew Currant of the Natural History Museum, London; Nigel Readman, keen ornithologist on the birds of the USSR; and Michael Wilson for his exceptionally generous, detailed and expert comments on the bird sequences; Susanna van Rose, geologist, for her willing and expert help on vulcanology for the chapter on Kamchatka; Sylva Rubashova for her inveterate kindness and helpfulness; the British Library, London Library and libraries of the Natural History Museum, Zoological Society, Royal Geographical Society and School of Slavonic Studies; my father, the late Hugh Stewart for his translation of the Gogol text in Chapter 4; Jane Gowman, above all, but also Jane Eker, Jackie Roberts and Jasper Dickinson for inputting the text and to all those who gave their help.

I must thank also the Survival Anglia cameramen and women credited herein for their first-hand accounts, as well as Petra Regent (producer of the television series), Chris Markham, Sue Flood and Kathryn Shreeve of Survival Anglia for their helpful advice and co-operation; Elaine Collins, Stephanie Walsh and particularly Penelope Cream, my editor at Boxtree, for her patience and faith in the author; my diligent and skilful copy-editor Richard Dawes; and any others inadvertently omitted.

Lastly, a warm, family thank you to my brother Michael and his wife Kathleen, for kindly checking the proofs, my sister, Margaret, for answering scientific queries, my daughter, Julia, for her excellent additional research, my son, Hamon for his ever-willing services as courier and chauffeur, and my unfailingly understanding and always supportive wife, Penelope, for her help in so very many ways as well as for her remarkable forbearance.

John Massey Stewart

CHAPTER ONE

THE LAND AND THE PEOPLE

It is both Europe and Asia, frozen tundra and scorching desert, snowcapped ranges and endless steppes, enormous rivers and the world's biggest forest. Ten time zones cross its 6000-mile (9660 km) expanse, a quarter of the globe's circumference. It borders Finland in the north-west and North Korea in the south-east, adjoining Poland and Romania, Iran and Afghanistan, Mongolia and China in between. Japan is only 100 miles (160 km) by sea from the mainland and 14 miles (22.5 km) from the southernmost of the Kuril Islands, America a mere 37 miles (60 km) away across the Bering Strait.

The USSR is a world in itself, but one which is at last opening its doors wide. The more the outsider travels through it, the more he is overwhelmed by the country's scale and contrasts: the number of different peoples and cultures, climates and ecosystems and the wide range of fauna and flora, including polar bear, sable and tiger, snow goose and Japanese crane, dwarf birch of the tundra and ginseng of the monsoon forest. Many of the species are to be found only in the Soviet Union and some are extremely rare, others endangered.

The climate, which the rest of the world firmly believes to be extremely cold, certainly embraces permafrost nearly a mile (1.5 km) deep that has never thawed since the last ice age and the northern pole of cold, with its average January temperature of −55 °F (−48.6 °C). But it also includes the blistering summer heat and searing winds of the Central Asian deserts, with average July temperatures of up to 90 °F (32.3 °C).

In prehistoric times the world's climate, vegetation and wildlife changed

The mountain slopes of the Caucasus form valleys which provide good grazing pastures for sheep.

markedly. Plants and animals spread in different directions, many over the most important two-way corridor, Beringia – the wide land-bridge across the present-day Bering Strait – which emerged and disappeared as the sea level rose and fell in successive ice ages. Large herds of hoofed mammals, including the bison, crossed from Siberia into North America as well as many species such as the mammoth and man, while the horse, camel and other animals crossed westwards into Siberia and therefore Eurasia. But with the ending of the ice ages, the pattern of today's flora and fauna was effectively set.

The earliest known evidence of man himself in what we know as the Soviet Union is surprisingly not in the fertile steppes, river systems or coastal areas of the more congenial south, but in the far north of Siberia, dating back, according to one controversial theory, as much as 2 million years, but certainly into palaeolithic times. About 20,000 years ago man was living in dwellings of mammoth bone and tusks both in Siberia and the Don basin of European Russia.

Around 5000 BC the first agriculture appeared in the extreme south of what is now Soviet Central Asia, and 2000 years later, agriculture reached European Russia independently, from the Danube region. Thus began a succession of agricultural societies living in permanent settlements, first in the wooded steppe and then gradually expanding northwards into the mixed forest. It was here that the Russian people developed: on this section of the vast plain which stretches all the way from northern France, across Russia, and halfway across the north of Asia, interrupted, astonishingly, only by the insignificant Urals, which are not really even mountains.

To understand the Russians' deep relationship with their land, we must look back several centuries. Many peoples crossed and recrossed the plains of eastern Europe and gradually, in about the seventh or eighth century AD, some of the eastern Slavs (as they became known) began to move from the Danube into what is now the Ukraine, settling in the valley of the River Dnieper, where they cultivated the fertile soil and found shelter and fuel, all available in the wooded steppe. From them the present-day Russians, Byelorussians and Ukrainians are descended. By the middle of the ninth century their scattered settlements had spread far to the north and eastwards to the Upper Volga.

Even at this early stage Russia's prodigious wildlife played a crucial role in its history. The abundance of fur-bearing animals was an obvious and easy source of tax, and in 859 AD the system of fur tribute began which was to last for nearly 1000 years, and greatly profit successive Russian governments. In that year both the Varangians (Swedish Vikings), who had arrived down the Dnieper, and the Khazars from Asia imposed tribute on the Slav tribes of 'a squirrel skin and beaver skin from each hearth'. But the Slavs rebelled and rejected their overlords and, to put it simply, appointed a Varangian, Rurik, as Prince of Kiev, which was by this time their capital. Rurik is known to history as the founder of Kievan Rus, the first Russian state.

The name 'Rus' may derive from 'Ruotsi', a Finnish name for the Swedes and probably a corruption of the Swedish 'Rothsmenn', meaning rowers or seafarers. It reflects the arrival of the Varangians by river to found the

Reindeer, essential to the lives of many northern peoples, are widely distributed over the vast area of the tundra and northern taiga.

nation that developed over 1000 years to become the Russian Empire and then the Soviet Union, and is now once more in a state of transformation.

However, the incohesive nature of Kievan Rus meant that it was unable to provide an adequate force to combat the nomadic bands from the east who were continually invading its southern lands. It was easier therefore to expand northwards into the forest-steppe, but then, in the thirteenth century, invasion by the Mongol–Tatar hordes and the sack of Kiev and many other towns, drove the Russians further north into the safety of the forests. The northern settlements of Novgorod, Vladimir and Moscow developed into towns and centres of government and trade. The merchants of Novgorod in particular prospered, by exploiting their large tracts of northern forest from which they obtained honey, wax, bark and, above all, furs for trade with foreign lands. By the eleventh century they had not only reached the White Sea but were organizing hunting on the islands of Novaya Zemlya in the Arctic Ocean.

To clear land for agricultural use, the Russians, like their Slav ancestors, used the slash-and-burn technique. They felled trees in spring and left them to lie until autumn. Then the trunks were trimmed and hauled away, leaving the branches and twigs to be burned the following spring and their ashes left on the ground. The early farmers did not till the ground, merely scattering seed and then covering it with soil, often using branches as rakes. In a couple of years the soil lost its fertility and then the whole low-yielding process would be repeated elsewhere, the worked-out land being left to revert to forest. Animal husbandry itself was always regarded as of secondary importance to finding enough fodder to feed livestock through the long, harsh winter.

It was the forest, however, which yielded most of man's needs: animals and birds for the pot, bark for shoes, wax for candles, hides for leather, and honey for consumption (and trade) as well as furs, not only for trade and paying taxes but also for the warm clothes that were essential in winter. Birds and small animals were snared or netted, and larger animals were caught with great nets hung from trees or hunted with hounds. Prince Vladimir Monomakh, Grand Prince of Kiev (1113–25) records hunting bison, boar, elk, stag and wild horses, all of which have long since disappeared from the region's forests. Russia's oldest crown, the famous 'Monomakh Cap', reputedly Vladimir's and made of gold and gold-lace filigree set with pearls and precious stones, is trimmed with a band of sable, which at that time inhabited the forests well west of Siberia. It is interesting that, even in the twelfth century, the preservation of game was regarded as important by the rulers and hunting strictly controlled by law. Each landowner had his own hunting preserve and there were harsh consequences for anyone who trespassed on another's preserve or interfered with his hounds, nets or snares.

But if the Russians hunted the animals, so they were hunted in turn, and far more inexorably, by plagues of tormenting mosquitoes in summer and in winter by fleas and plague-bearing lice. The latter must have caused much ill temper as they found refuge from the cold in the badly cured furs and unsavoury woollens of hapless peasant and prince alike. Foreign visitors to medieval Muscovy, the principality based on Moscow, often commented on the wealthy's magnificent furs – and lice.

The compensation for the severe climate was the number of fur-bearing animals adapted to it: at that time a huge population of sable, beaver, black fox, otter and many other species. Fortunately for the Russian exchequer, fur became fashionable in medieval times, and the country's furs proved by far the most valuable of its commodities, usually obtained from the (often hostile) native peoples of the forest as tribute, though not without friction. There was a ready market for Russian furs not only in northern and western Europe but throughout the Islamic lands and even China. The Russian traders from the northern cities often took the pelts to their markets by long, complex routes by land, sea, river and portage, which suggests that they expected a handsome return when they bartered them for silks, spices and all manner of other goods.

The Mongol invasion and the destruction of Kiev, Vladimir, Moscow and many other cities encouraged the Russians to move north into the safety of the forests. Novgorod almost alone escaped, protected by the surrounding marshes, which proved impassable to the Asiatic horsemen, and indeed continued, exceptionally, to prosper and expand its influence.

The fur trade south to the Black Sea may have been interrupted by the Mongols, but there were ever-increasing demands from the countries of the Scandinavian region and throughout Europe, even though fashions in fur changed. Twelfth-century German princes, for instance, switched from sable to grey squirrel fur, which became fashionable both for trimming the new, woollen cloth then all the rage and for costly fur linings for luxurious winter garments made of hundreds of small pelts, carefully trimmed and matched.

The various shades of spruce, larch, birch and fir merge along the banks of one of the rivers of the taiga, the largest forest in the world.

Henry III and Edward I of England both preferred squirrel to sable, and 'filled their wardrobes mainly with northern squirrel', while Edward III's Queen Philippa ensured that the fashion for squirrel continued well into the fourteenth century. So fashionable was fur that wealthy merchants invested their savings in it. Indeed so popular did it become that in 1327, presumably to preserve some exclusivity, it was decreed that only members of royalty and those of high birth were allowed to wear fur-trimmed garments. Later laws conceded that the nobility, clergy and wealthy citizens could wear imported furs, but the northern grey squirrel was reserved for the wealthiest knights and those of higher rank.

In only six years Henry V amassed '625 sable pelts, two sable linings, 20,000 pelts and 113 linings of marten'. Henry VI preferred marten and bought only grey squirrel for court dependants. Henry VII reverted to sable, and Henry VIII is reported to have had one gown of damask and velvet with 80 sable pelts and another of black satin with 350 sable pelts.

All this time the Novgorod merchants were expanding their empire. As they acquired land — a huge tract on one river was purchased with ten Novgorodian roubles and 20,000 squirrel pelts — they made sure that the valuable hunting rights were part of the estate deeds. By the fourteenth

Steam from an erupting crater rises from one of the snow-capped volcanoes of the Kamchatka peninsula which projects into the North Pacific.

century Novgorod's influence had penetrated east beyond the Urals well into Siberia.

But Muscovy, which was paying the Tatars fur tribute, attacked Novgorod in 1456, demanding possession of two of its northern colonies with their great fur assets, and in 1570, Ivan the Terrible (1530–84) was able to subdue Novgorod and acquire all its lands.

In 1552 Ivan had seized the Tatar khanate of Kazan on the Volga, enabling Russian expansion eastwards, primarily in search of furs. As one stretch of forest after another was cleared of its fur-bearing animals, so the Russians – most often Cossack adventurers – pushed onwards through Siberia. As they proceeded by river and portage through the endless taiga and occasional wooded steppe, they subjugated the native peoples – hunters, fishermen and herders of reindeer and livestock – imposing the inexorable fur tribute.

By 1639 they had crossed the 3100 miles (5000 km) from the Urals to the Pacific, their incentive being the pelts, which were taken all the way back to Moscow. Although both the quantity and quality of available fur-bearers were fast diminishing, Ivan the Terrible was able to send a handsome present of sable pelts to Elizabeth I of England in 1567. (In the present century, Khrushchev, when visiting Britain as Russian leader, presented a sable coat to Elizabeth II.)

During the next two centuries, ranging over the seemingly limitless lands, the Russians amassed a territory stretching to the Pacific, an empire nearly two and a half times the size of the United States. Across this vast terrain they encountered an extraordinary variety of landscape and wildlife. To the

Patterns formed by the snow on Wrangel Island in the Arctic Ocean.

east they found the endless taiga; to the south the wide, open steppe with its coarse grasses, so difficult to break with the plough, as they were to discover. It was of little consolation that in spring the green gave way to a myriad of hues as flowers burst into bloom and covered the land like a multi-coloured carpet. They also came upon a great variety of birds both on the steppe and in the taiga, and herds of game animals apart from the ever-desirable sable and its kin.

The Russians found that the belt of forest-steppe, with its rich, black soil, stretched across the country to Siberia's River Ob and beyond. This was the chernozem, the exceptionally fertile black earth which lies between the northern forests and the open steppe to the south. Its Ukrainian section in particular has been coveted by many peoples, including the Poles and Lithuanians and, during the Second World War, the Germans.

North of this rich belt of potentially arable land the settlers found that the mixed forests of European Russia continued in a huge swath eastwards, merging into the great coniferous forest for thousands of miles and then, near the River Amur, changing again into a totally different, northern monsoon forest with unfamiliar animals including leopards, tigers and exotic birds. They must have been astounded by the geysers in the far north-east, but even more so by the active volcanoes of the Kamchatka peninsula and the Kuril Islands.

North of the taiga lay the belt of tundra, seemingly empty and desolate, with no trees higher than dwarf shrubs, and with its permafrost beneath them. But they soon found it was home to the reindeer, Arctic fox and lemming as well as vast numbers of waterfowl and other birds. Even further north, on the edge of the frozen ocean, they discovered polar bears and sea mammals.

In the nineteenth century, expanding southwards, Russia annexed both Transcaucasia, with its high mountains and subtropical coasts, and the semi-desert and desert proper of Islamic Central Asia, with its historic cities of Samarkand and Bokhara, fringed by the spectacular Tien Shan range – the Mountains of Heaven – rising to 24,400 ft (7439 m) and the Pamirs, with a maximum height of 24,600 ft (7495 m). The twentieth century has seen further accretions under Stalin, particularly that of the Baltic states on the western border, which had once been part of the Czarist Empire.

And thus the largest country in the world has come into existence, with its 130 or so disparate ethnic groups and its enormous range of habitats and wildlife – so disparate are these peoples that 'Russia' may be a convenient term but very inaccurate. It was, however, the Russians who began to settle in Siberia, and as the forts which the Cossacks had built across the wilderness quickly developed into towns, Russia's search for fur brought rapid colonization right across the country. By contrast, in Canada, with its comparable fur resources, settlers preferred the less rigorous climate of the south-east and the eastern seaboard, and as they gradually moved across the country, they kept to the southern strip of cultivable land, only the itinerant trapper and trader venturing north. (Even as late as the 1940s Ontario schoolchildren were taught that two thirds of their land had nine months of snow and ice a year and that it was virtually impossible to survive in the Arctic wastes.) But the Russians came to terms early with their harsh, northern environment and learned from the local peoples how to live off the taiga, tundra and Arctic coastline, relying on reindeer, fish and sea mammals for most of their needs.

It has been argued that Russia's northerly location has militated against it. If it had been a few degrees further south, it is said, its fortunes would have been very different, for in its present position much otherwise cultivable land lies too far north for farming. But if Russia had lain further south its size and distance from the moderating effects of any ocean (apart from the Pacific) would have brought the problems of an extreme continental climate. A factor that has limited fertility is the location of Russia's mountains, around its southern edges and Siberia, which tends to restrict precipitation to limited areas and in the wrong season. As a result, dry, hot winds blow across huge areas, baking the land and blowing away the topsoil.

Although the territory and its resources must have seemed limitless, the first protection of wild birds and animals dates from the eleventh century in Kieven Rus. In 1667 Tsar Aleksei Mikhailovich issued a decree on hunting and the conservation of game (not just the sable), ordering particularly that a certain coastal area be set aside for the protection of the gyrfalcon's nesting grounds.

His son, Peter the Great, as usual far ahead of his time, understood better than any other Tsar the need to preserve natural resources. He introduced forest management and conservation, mainly to protect the valuable fur-bearing animals like sable and beaver, but also the elk which was being heavily over-hunted. He ordered timber firms to divide their forest holdings

The inquisitive gaze of a young brown bear. Brown bear cubs emerge from the den, where they are born, after two or three months and remain with their mothers until half-grown.

into some thirty sections and cut only one a year. He also had the foresight to maintain wide forest zones along river banks, forbidding any felling within a 33 mile (53 km) belt along major rivers and 13 miles (21 km) along minor ones – significantly, a greater protected area than today. In addition, he brought in laws against overfishing, for this was rapidly depleting fish stocks, and introduced pollution controls for the waterways of St Petersburg.

It was Peter who carried out the first afforestation programmes in the southern steppe, and he was very aware of the importance of forests in flood prevention and as a measure against erosion. These early conservation measures were bolstered by the threat of harsh punishment for transgressors. A number of enlightened landowners followed the Tsar's example, introducing hunting and tree-felling restrictions on their vast estates.

But unfortunately Peter the Great's forest laws were not properly enforced in the following reigns, and Catherine the Great (1762–96) rescinded them. She was, however, concerned to preserve wildlife – perhaps

merely to ensure there was enough to hunt – and banned hunting in the breeding season between the beginning of March and the end of June.

What impressed many foreign travellers of the time was the amount of wildlife. A Scottish doctor, John Bell, travelling across Russia to Peking in 1719, noted that in Siberia 'are various kinds of wild beasts; such as bears, wolves, lynxes, several sorts of foxes, squirrels, ermine, sables, martins . . .'. He reported also the great number of freshwater fish and the presence of elk, reindeer and roebuck, as well as 'an incredible number of hares, which . . . are generally caught by the country people . . . and the skins sent, in great quantities to St Petersburg, and other ports, in order to be exported to England, Holland, and other countries; where they are chiefly manufactured into hats'. Further south, in the fertile western Siberian wooded steppe, Bell found the local people growing 'wheat, rye, barley, oats, and other grains'.

Despite the apparently inexhaustible supply of game and other animals, the advancing Russians in the newly claimed lands of Siberia had a devastating effect on the local wildlife, and the local peoples who had hunted from time immemorial with spears, bows and arrows and nets, themselves began to acquire guns from the Russians. In many areas the sable became almost extinct and the sea otter and fur seal of the northern Pacific were ruthlessly destroyed by both Russian and American hunters in the name of money and fashion, despite the objections of the native peoples that killing the breeding animals would wipe out the species.

Nineteenth-century Russia saw a rapid growth in the commercial exploitation of natural resources and the beginnings of industrialization. Whole forests were felled and inevitably the surviving wildlife fled. The numbers of elk, for instance, fell drastically. The Forest Protection Law introduced in 1888 was already too late to prevent serious erosion in some regions, and bad agricultural practices speeded the soil's depletion in vulnerable areas.

Towards the end of the century, prominent Russian scientists, concerned about man's assault on nature, pressed for a system of nature reserves. In 1916 the first law concerning these was passed, and by the time of the 1917 Revolution six reserves had been established. With the sable now almost facing extinction, one of these reserves was created on the east coast of Lake Baikal to protect the Barguzin sable, the most valuable subspecies; and with a general prohibition on sable hunting, the animal (not just the Barguzin subspecies) recovered and has now recolonized its former forests. Today the Barguzin reserve covers 1016 square miles (2 632 sq km) and protects not only the sable but 38 other species of mammal, including the famous freshwater seal of Baikal, four species of reptiles, two of amphibians, 243 of birds, and 600 of flowering plants – as well as hot springs.

Despite the turmoil that followed the Revolution, the new regime addressed the question of nature conservation remarkably early. More than 200 rules and regulations on the subject came into being between 1917 and 1922 alone. In 1919 and 1920, while civil war was still raging, the first two post-revolutionary nature reserves were established, in the Astrakhan delta and at Ilmen in the southern Urals. Unusually, the object of this latter reserve was to protect not specific animals or plants but minerals, for the Europe–Asia divide is of particular geological interest, with its 260 minerals,

The white whooper swans of the Volga delta and their tawny cygnets. Named after their bugle-like call, the swans live beside the dense rushes of the delta banks and migrate further south during the harsh winter.

19

ABOVE *Yak-cattle are often encountered on the slopes of the Caucasus. A crossbreed between domestic yak and cattle, the females are generally fertile and the males infertile.*

BELOW *The lynx, with its distinctive pointed ears and magnificent coat, is a keen predator, feeding off deer, foxes, rabbits and small rodents.*

ranging from copper to opal. During the Second World War, despite the USSR's desperate need for minerals of all kinds, the reserve remained fully protected, although tree-felling was allowed but with saplings carefully protected to ensure regrowth.

In 1921, two years after the Ilmen reserve was established, Lenin set up the State Committee for the Conservation of Nature. Over the following decades reserves embraced tundra, taiga, steppe, desert, mountain and indeed all the habitats and most important natural sites of the USSR. But progress has not been steady. In 1951 two-thirds of the reserves, or *zapovedniki*, were abolished, and although their number increased again in the 1950s there was a further reduction in 1961.

However, the number of reserves has grown again, and by 1990 there were about 160 of up to 3860 square miles (10,000 sq km), with a total area of 85,000 square miles (220,000 sq km). At least 22 reserves are devoted to

Crested auklets on Talan Island in the North Pacific. These diving birds have brightly coloured plates on their bills which are shed after the breeding season. The plates emit an odour similar to that of tangerines.

preserving specific rare or endangered fauna such as the polar bear, Siberian crane, steppe marmot and snow leopard. Most of them have their own small natural history museums and research laboratories, where scientists work in a protected environment generally prohibited to visitors and human activity and therefore in an optimum natural state. As of 1988, 19 had been accepted as 'Biosphere Reserves' under UNESCO's Man and the Biosphere programme, which combines nature conservation and scientific research.

Most *zapovedniki* are in European Russia, and many of these are in the Caucasus because of its extraordinary variety of landscape, climate, plants and animals. The first reserve in the far north was established in 1932 at Kandalaksha, near Murmansk on the Kola peninsula, to protect 550 species of Arctic plants, 210 of birds and 33 of mammals. In 1975 it became part of a much larger area on the White Sea which is now officially a wetlands area of internationally recognised importance.

An important development in Arctic conservation occurred in 1979, when an area of tundra on the Taimyr peninsula, two thirds the size of Wales at 5200 square miles (13,483 sq km), became the largest *zapovednik* in the USSR, although it has been superseded since by the great Lena delta. The Taimyr reserve protects a host of wildlife, particularly the rare red-breasted goose (*Branta ruficollis*), which breeds only in Siberia. Even more remote is the unique reserve of Wrangel Island in the Arctic Ocean, which protects polar bears, walruses, snow geese and the rare Ross's roseate gull.

According to Philip M. Pryde, a leading American expert on Soviet environmental management, 'the Soviet *zapovedniki* system is recognized as one of the world's most important nature reserve networks'.

In addition, covering more than twice the total area of the *zapovedniki*, are nearly 3000 *zakazniki* or reserves with protection limited (sometimes on a temporary basis) to certain species or seasons. They may, for instance, protect rare flora or particular animals in the breeding season, with farming or limited activities allowed the rest of the year. According to each sanctuary's importance, it is either guarded by a resident warden or visited by an itinerant warden in a jeep. There exists also a relatively new national park system. The first park was established in Estonia in 1971 and there are now 16 of them in ten of the USSR's republics, and three is the newly independent Baltic States, allowing visitors and certain economic activities.

The whole system of protected areas is of growing importance, especially in the fragile Arctic environment, where extraction of the rich natural resources, at present particularly gas, has brought massive degradation. The construction of buildings, roads and railways and the extraction of minerals cause irreparable harm to the delicate tundra. Gas pipelines have barred the reindeer's migration routes. The arrival of men and equipment and the ensuing disturbance have in many places badly affected the lives of both the native peoples and wildlife. Man has corrupted some animals such as the Arctic fox, elk and reindeer in that they now often move closer to human settlements for easy pickings. In many places human activity has unwittingly destabilized the permafrost, with disastrous consequences. The heat from large buildings, for instance, thaws the permafrost beneath, so they are now built on piles sunk into the frozen ground – but with unknown long-term effects.

While the permafrost is the most sensitive of all the USSR's ecosystems, the

A rapid mountain stream passing through one of the geyser valleys of Kamchatka.

others have suffered from the massive economic expansion that has taken place under the Soviet regime. The guiding concept had long been that nature has limitless resources and is to be conquered, and this outlook has been bolstered by the inefficiencies and absurdities of an ideologically based command economy administered from a distant, bureaucratic capital.

Furthermore, the whole of the country effectively had to justify itself economically. The marginal steppe lands of Kazakhstan and southern Siberia were ploughed and put under grain in an effort to raise food production, but with some dire consequences. Although fast-growing strains are now sown in the short, hot summers of these regions, much soil has been depleted in the process or alternatively has been so over-fertilized that the local rivers and lands have become seriously polluted.

Many waterways have been seriously polluted for decades, and whereas in the eighteenth century John Bell exclaimed at the abundance of fish, now in many parts of the Soviet Union they have declined substantially in size, numbers or both and it is sometimes hazardous to eat them.

From its early days in power the Soviet government was well aware of the need to conserve resources, the better to exploit them. Over the decades a multitude of agencies was set up at central government and republic levels to oversee various aspects of pollution control and the protection of land resources. But, unconnected, uncoordinated and often with onerous economic functions to perform, they failed to cope. In an effort to coordinate this typically Soviet bureaucratic nightmare, the Central Directorate for the Conservation of Nature, Natural Preserves and Hunting Economy of the Ministry of Agriculture of the USSR was set up in 1965.

Nonetheless, the state plan's production targets remained paramount in any conflict with nature. Siberia's revered Lake Baikal, the world's largest body of fresh water, became the Soviet Union's first environmental *cause célèbre* when industry began to pollute it – a problem unresolved to this day. For many years both scientists and writers have campaigned to save Baikal, the writers acting as the voice of the people in an autocratic state. And the growing public outcry, now possible under glasnost, against the despoiling of air, soil, water – and health – has given birth to a mass of local green movements across the country as well as many protests and demonstrations.

Before glasnost and perestroika, the state's restrictions on information and open discussion meant that events such as the 1957 nuclear accident at Kyshtym in the Urals, and indeed any disaster, was a state secret, creating a hotbed for rumours. Indeed Kyshtym was not officially acknowledged until 30 years later. However, the nuclear accident at Chernobyl in 1986 was a major catalyst of glasnost and brought home the scale of man-made disasters and mismanagement.

In the present era of almost totally free speech, the public has become increasingly well informed and concerned about the grave environmental problems across the country: air, water and radioactive pollution, degradation of the landscape, and the severe consequences for health and life expectancy and for nature as a whole. Since Chernobyl the Soviet media has been full of the environmental situation: facts, figures, exposés, horror stories, experts' opinions. Chernobyl apart, the most serious disaster is that in Central Asia. Here the Aral Sea has shrunk catastrophically as a

result of the diversion of its inflowing rivers into irrigation systems for the extensive cotton fields. There is now a major problem not only of salinization but of a water supply poisoned by pesticides and the huge doses of fertilizer necessitated by growing nothing but cotton continuously year after year.

Another problem, among many, is the effect of the great hydroelectric schemes for which valuable land and resources have been drowned, the microclimate adversely affected and fish prevented by the dams from reaching their spawning grounds, with huge losses of stocks.

One root cause of the present environmental situation may well be the historical relationship of the Russians with their land. In Tsarist times, settlers in the forest-steppe and steppe proper worked their land in the same wasteful way as their slash-and-burn brothers further north, exploiting the land until it was exhausted, then moving on elsewhere, leaving an

Polar bears play-fighting. The polar bear is found along the Russian Arctic coast to the Bering Straits and is now protected under an international conservation programme.

This mammoth tusk was recovered from a mud bank in the Kolyma region of north eastern Siberian where it had been trapped in the permafrost.

impoverished environment behind them. Even in European Russia the peasants were careless in the use of their land. But then it did not belong to them anyway, at least not until the abolition of serfdom in 1862. Even then, it was not theirs; it had to be purchased, and if the peasants could not meet the payments as they fell due, they would usually have to move off the land or work for a more successful farmer. Most landlords, too, had little interest in their estates, and few took the trouble to manage them properly, let alone improve them or increase output. Yet such was the fertility of the steppe's famous black-earth belt and the ability of the larger estates to continue to extract produce from the peasantry that there were massive grain and dairy exports before the First World War.

The sheer size of the USSR and its seemingly limitless resources may be at the root of its environmental problems. History may well have taught the Russians to love their motherland passionately but it has not taught them to care for it. And any relationship they may have had with the land – so much weaker than that of their counterparts in overcrowded, Europe with its different history – was effectively destroyed by the collectivization of agriculture from 1928. Land had been nationalized in 1917 and given to the peasants, only to be collectivized, together with livestock, in the 1930s, causing the end of any commitment to the soil.

In an effort to boost agricultural production, vast areas of virgin steppe were ploughed under the early Five-Year Plans but, unlike the black earth further north, the steppe is not naturally fertile and its crops are at the mercy of an unpredictable climate which can often produce an unseasonably cold snap at planting time or summer rains at harvest time that ruin the crops. And as larger areas came under the plough, the problems of erosion increased.

The pattern was repeated from 1954 when Khrushchev, looking for more land on which to grow grain to feed the people, sent thousands of enthusiastic young volunteers to bring into production huge areas of virgin steppe, particularly in Kazakhstan. For centuries the grazing grounds for the herds and flocks of the semi-nomadic Kazakhs, this land was now destined to be the new corn belt – like the prairies of North America.

Today only a tiny vestige of the great steppe remains in its virgin state, and that within nature reserves. It is to be hoped that irresponsible exploitation of the environment is now on the wane, although it still continues, for instance in the timber industry. The environmentally aware are still in the minority but the conservation movement is growing, albeit a decade or so later than in the West, and there are many positive signs. For instance, the Soviet Union is prominent in international wildlife protection and the breeding of rare species. It collaborates internationally in many environmental matters and in 1978 published the most comprehensive of all the national Red Data Books of rare and endangered species, and then a new and enlarged edition in 1985 in two volumes, one for fauna, one for flora.

Many leading scientists work to conserve these species, while important research institutes across the country study countless ecological subjects. The recently formed state environmental committee, Goskompriroda, with its republican and regional branches, has now been upgraded to the Ministry of Natural Resources Management and Environmental Protection (Minpriroda). Headed, significantly, by the first minister not to be a Communist party member Prof. Nikolay N. Vorontsov, its role is to tackle the many urgent problems throughout the USSR.

However, despite man's continuing onslaught on Nature, he can also be its prey. The environment of the USSR's far north can be particularly hostile. Here a distinct world exists – of no trees, permanently frozen soil, midnight sun and polar night and an astonishing range of animals with their closely woven relationships. This world is the tundra.

CHAPTER TWO

THE VAST SPACE OF THE TUNDRA

Endless space. Empty except for the hordes of lemmings and the polar foxes, wolves, reindeer and birds. And everywhere rivers, lakes, pools, bogs and peaty hummocks: the wettest landscape on earth because there is virtually no evaporation or absorption into the frozen subsoil. In the short summer of the midnight sun it is a carpet of colour. But in winter it becomes a bleak and frozen Arctic night with ferocious blizzards and average temperatures down to −31 °F (−35 °C) and snow cover lasting in places up to nine months, although, rather surprisingly, only 20 in (50 cm) deep at most when level.

This is the tundra, which rings the earth's northernmost land masses of North America and Eurasia between the great coniferous forest belts and the Arctic coastlines, along which are occasional patches of polar desert. It is a remarkable habitat: rock-hard in winter yet in summer so fragile that even a footprint may leave a scar. The word 'tundra' comes from the Finnish *tunturi*, meaning treeless heights. For, besides the moss, lichen and 500-odd species of low-growing flowering plants, only stunted willows, birches, alders and dwarf shrubs can survive in the intensely bitter winds of winter and the brief summer's 4–5 in (10–12 cm) of thawed out, acid soil (where there is neither bog nor stony, gravelly tundra). And below that insubstantial layer – a plant carpet soft and spongy underfoot – lies permafrost up to 3300 ft (1000 m) deep, ground which may have been permanently frozen since the last ice age.

Extending southwards well into the taiga or coniferous forest, the permafrost zone has never had a chance to thaw because for most of the year

Reindeer skins provide warm winter clothing for the northern peoples. This man is wearing a loose reindeer-leather coat, or malitsa, *and* kisy, *soft-soled reindeer-fur boots.*

the average monthly temperature is well below freezing point, even though in the farthest north the temperature can reach 68 °F (20 °C) in July.

It is the world's biggest fridge after the frozen parts of Antarctica. In summer, locals keep perishable foodstuffs fresh in holes in the ground, and when the naturalist Sir Peter Scott and his family visited the Yamal peninsula in 1978, 'For food we had brought a reindeer carcass, which was buried under the tundra turf on the surface of the permafrost'.

The tundra can be a forbidding place. The polar night reigns from November to February with only the occasional glow of the Aurora Borealis (Northern Lights) to brighten the darkness. Temperatures may descend to −58 °F (−50 °C) and in winter the fierce *purga* blows from the north or north-east, driving snow and ice particles before it at gale force.

Although hard frosts may last until May, and blizzards, even frost, until mid June, usually by mid May there are signs of spring and the thaw comes to at least the southern tundra. Summer temperatures can soar in July, and then drop sharply in August. But on the southern Taimyr peninsula the temperature remains below freezing for nearly eight months of the year. One Soviet anthropologist, A. A. Popov, studying the Nganasany people there, noted that:

> spring comes suddenly, and the snow melts very quickly. Since the polar day has a lot of heat, the tundra blossoms out in bright colours in the shortest possible time, and silent, dead winter is abruptly brought back to life by the cries of great flocks of birds. The unusual hardiness of the vivid polar flowers is astonishing. I remember that in August, despite the coming of cold and snow, the slopes of the Northeastern Plateau were still thickly covered with bright blue Alpine forget-me-nots (*Myosotis alpestris*).

In the summer a spectacular carpet of flowering plants – pinks, Arctic poppies, gentians, delphiniums, among others – replaces the endless white of winter, and the tundra comes to life with Arctic fox, wolf, 'tundra' partridge, lemming, reindeer, and millions of gnats, midges and mosquitoes in the endless bogs.

This strange and inhospitable realm of tundra stretches across the entire north of the USSR, from the Finnish border to the Bering Strait, some 4350 miles (7000 km) to the east. It varies in width from less than 50 miles (80 km) in the far west to 420 miles (670 km) on the Taimyr peninsula, the northernmost point of all Eurasia. The total area of 1.2 million square miles (3.1 million sq km) – almost that of India – accounts for nearly 15 percent of the Soviet Union.

Tens of millions of years ago thick coniferous forests grew in this area, judging from pieces of amber, formed from the resin of conifers, which have been found along the Arctic coast and almost at the mouth of the river Lena. Here were great tropical forests of the carboniferous period which formed rich reserves of coal, oil and gas. It was some 26 million years ago, in the mid-Tertiary period, that vegetation first appeared on the tundra.

The geological formation of the tundra has produced a wealth of mineral deposits, and indeed northern Siberia has been called a 'frozen Eldorado'. For here lies an unimaginable wealth of copper, nickel, tin, cobalt, platinum,

coal (six billion tonnes of it on the Taimyr peninsula alone), gold and diamonds.

In the present century these riches have brought about an invasion of the Russian tundra far greater than that of the North American tundra across the Arctic Ocean. It began in the Stalin era when around a million slave labourers were ruthlessly dragooned into extracting the country's mineral wealth, much of it in the tundra, with terrible mortality. Permanent settlements – indeed towns – have grown up, among them Vorkuta (pop. 104,000, 1982), based on the area's coal reserves, which are bigger than those of the Donbass. (One of the region's mines has Europe's largest output capacity.) The biggest urban concentration lies on the Taimyr peninsula, Norilsk and its satellites, the largest town in the world north of the Arctic circle (pop. 280,000, 1990), founded in 1922 to exploit the huge local reserves of copper, nickel, cobalt and coal, some extracted from vast open-cast pits.

In the 1960s oil and gas were found in the tundra just east of the Urals, part of the western Siberian plain's immensely rich deposits. The result has been the arrival of men, machinery, vehicles and aircraft, with consequent disruption, environmental degradation and decline of wildlife. The electric power lines overhead, for instance, have caused mass mortality among migratory birds. The many hundreds of miles of pipelines now crossing the tundra have also brought problems. Unfortunately, some were built across reindeer migration routes so that when the reindeer encountered the new

The delicate surface of the tundra is in parts scored with tracks as a result of economic and industrial development. Melting the permafrost, the tracks may take at least a decade to disappear.

The Nentsy people move across the tundra with their reindeer herd which helps transport the box-like house, or balok, *mounted on a sledge and covered with reindeer pelts.*

barriers they milled around confused until they died by the thousand from lack of fodder. Since then sections of pipelines across the traditional routes have been raised to allow the reindeer to pass beneath. In the beginning the reindeer were uneasy, but gradually adjusted.

Palaeoasiatic man first arrived in this tundra in prehistoric times, probably following the retreat of the ice. Now, besides the mainly Russian immigrants, almost entirely of the twentieth century, who have come principally to extract the mineral wealth, there are nine distinct native peoples, totalling some 650,000, who have lived in the tundra since time immemorial, their lifestyle adapted to the harsh natural conditions and based on their dependence on and understanding of nature. Here, from west to east live Komi, Nentsy, Nganasany, Dolgany, Yakuts, Eveny, Chukchi, Koryaks and Eskimos, each with their own distinct culture and language, although many are under severe pressure from the impact of development and their languages are declining because of the lingua franca of Russian.

These peoples still predominantly live off the land, sea and rivers by catching fish, hunting sea mammals or herding the tundra and taiga's 2.2 million domesticated reindeer. The Soviet Union is in fact the only country with a highly developed tradition of reindeer husbandry. Besides the domesticated herds, however, there are some 900,000 wild reindeer (*Rangifer tarandus*), 'caribou' in North America, of which there are six subspecies. The biggest herd, on the Taimyr peninsula, numbers at least 430,000. In addition there are tens of thousands of feral reindeer which have escaped from the domestic herds. The total number therefore approaches 4 million, the world's biggest reindeer population and two thirds of the world's total.

In summer the reindeer are particularly fond of the lichen known as reindeer moss (*Cladonia rangiferina*), but they also eat other tundra grasses and plants. In winter they break the snow crust with their hooves to feed on the moss and lichen which they can smell beneath. Smaller animals are able to shelter beneath the snow, yet this big mammal can survive when the air temperature drops to −58 °F (−50 °C) and winds are of hurricane force. How does it do it? In winter the tips of its hairs grow thicker, making it far harder for winds to penetrate. Its legs may have less hair than its body and fall in temperature to below 50 °F (10 °C), but they do not freeze, because of the chemical properties of its body tissue. But the reindeer also has three other unique characteristics. Since grazing is often difficult in winter, it is adapted – rather like the camel in the waterless desert – to live on its reserves and it can safely lose a fifth of its muscles. It can also survive through the long Arctic winter on a totally saltless diet of snow and Iceland moss. And finally it has three lungs, the third acting, it is thought, as an extra internal heater.

Probably the first attempts to domesticate reindeer took place about 7000 years ago in southern Siberia east of Lake Baikal. Documents of China's Tang dynasty (618–907 AD) record that the tribes of this region 'keep reindeer in the manner of cattle or horses. These animals subsist only on moss . . .'. It was the reindeer, an easily tamed and herded animal, which allowed man to settle in the otherwise impossible tundra. It provided all his needs: shelter, food and drink, transport and essential artefacts. Its hide provided wigwams (here called 'chums'), its pelt clothes and footwear, its tendons thread and string, its bones and antlers all necessary implements. The Nganasany would use bullets smeared with rancid reindeer fat to act as a poison. Even reindeer excrement was used, mixed with fat, to waterproof any cracks in their dugout canoes. The peoples of western Siberia, to stop their skis sliding the wrong way, still attach to the underside the pelt from the reindeer's legs, using a strong waterproof glue made from a sturgeon's swim-bladder.

So totally bound to the reindeer are these northern peoples that the Nganasany, who were not collectivized until 1952, traditionally had their own reindeer-and-nature-based calendar year, divided into somewhat indefinite lunar months as the moon was not always visible through snowstorms and other adverse conditions. For the Nganasany there were two years: a winter and a summer year. The eight-month winter year included a cold month when the female reindeer, no longer suckling her young, shivered with cold. The summer year had only four months, which included a first fawn's and a last fawn's month. How did the Nganasany know if it was morning on days of fog or cloud in the Arctic summer's perpetual daylight? Simply by knowing if their domesticated reindeer had eaten twice during the 'night', as they always did.

Today the herdsmen may have radios in their 'chums' and have the best pastures located for them from the air, and even, albeit exceptionally, spend holidays on the Black Sea or the Bulgarian riviera. But they still wear in winter their indispensable *kisy* and *malitsy*, respectively long soft-soled reindeer-fur boots, and loose, ankle-length reindeer-leather coats (with the fur inside) with sewn-in gloves and tight fur hoods. They know that clad in these they can sleep on the snow even in a severe frost and not freeze. And when not in the settlements attached to the 150 state and collective reindeer-breeding farms, they still live in their practical 'chums', which need only a few minutes to pack up.

The Dolgans of the southern Taimyr peninsula ride their reindeer or use them as pack animals in summer and as sled teams in winter with herd dogs supplied by their neighbours, the Nganasany, at a high price. The dogs are the short-legged, white Arctic samoyed, which, with the lesser-known malemut, are the only tundra species to be adopted outside the USSR. The Dolgans own reindeer for transport only, living entirely by hunting, whereas the Nentsy, the first to develop reindeer husbandry – that is, the production of reindeer meat – have big herds in order to trade meat, which only they and the Chukchi do.

Up to 25,000 tons of reindeer meat are now sold annually in the USSR as fresh, frozen or tinned meat. Perhaps the great herds are one answer to the country's present food shortage. In addition, the pelts and hides now provide warm clothes for the local populace as well as the native peoples. (Between the two world wars, Russia exported up to 20,000 reindeer hides to Britain each year for gloves and handbags.)

Wild reindeer no longer exist in Dolgan and Nentsy areas, for since wild stags steal does from the domesticated herds, the reindeer herders have shot them *en masse* whenever they have come across them. On the Nentsy's Yamal peninsula, therefore, wild reindeer survive only in the very far north, which almost no domesticated herds reach. The rest of the Yamal provides huge grazing areas for the domesticated herds, despite the natural-gas development, and the Nentsy's way of life is integrated with the reindeer in every detail.

It is an impressive and highly developed reindeer culture and economy where everything has its use. Thus, from reindeer herders' belts, with their decorative copper buckles, hang many small objects made of mammoth bone, each for a specific purpose. For instance, one is used to undo knots in frozen whips and, as a Russian says who knows the Nentsy well, 'It is constructed so perfectly that no designer could produce a better instrument. It's pure genius! The Nentsy have a great culture which no one's yet really studied.'

In late July and early August the reindeer go almost mad, demented by the gadflies which swarm even at daybreak. For the reindeer herdsman this is the worst time of the year. His reindeer flee panic-stricken in all

The children are kept warmly insulated from the cold, their closed sleeves ensuring that hands are kept safely within the reindeer-fur coats.

directions into the distance and have to be retrieved by the dogs. But one trick at least the reindeer have mastered when thus pestered: they run ahead, then suddenly turn and lie down behind a large rock, while the outwitted gadflies fly on straight ahead. Fortunately, as the herdsmen move north and the weather cools, torment by gadfly decreases.

Such factors apart, the life of the wild reindeer is obviously different from that of the domesticated animal. It lives in small herds or, less often, singly, until the rutting season in late September or early October when the stags collect large herds of does and then prevent them leaving. During this rutting season the stags become extremely irritable. They run after does all day, fight fiercely with each other and can attack humans and indeed kill them by butting them with their newly ossified antlers, with which, aided by their hooves, they can sometimes fight off wolves. The herd instinct is so strong that if the herd leader is killed, the does will return several times to the spot to look for him.

Twice a year in spring and autumn the wild reindeer set off on their remarkable journeys of more than 620 miles (1000 km) to the north and then back, some reaching the Arctic coast. In 1986 2000 reindeer decided to head through the tundra's biggest town, Norilsk. Tens of miles of fences

Industrial change and traditional lifestyle come together as a Nentsy sledge passes a modern refinery in the tundra.

were erected to stop their entry and roads blocked to traffic to let them pass. It is during the wild herds' autumn migration that special hunting collectives gather at river crossings on the migration routes to kill a designated number for meat to be supplied to the state. In the pre-collectivization days these reindeer slaughtering places were considered sacred as well as the property of individual clans.

In those old days every Nenets knew the tundra from the mouth of the Pechora, west of the Urals, to the River Yenisei – a distance of some 1500 miles (2400 km) – and they would lead their herds along different routes according to the snow cover. If, for instance, there had been little snowfall and the spring was normal, one clan would lead its herds across the frozen River Ob to summer pastures in the central Yamal. But if there had been heavy snow they would make a long detour to avoid the southern Yamal, where the snow is particularly deep and they could easily lose their reindeer. Instead they would make a great circuit east and then north across the next peninsula and its frozen gulf on to the following (Gydansk) peninsula and turn west across the frozen Ob bay, 9 miles (15 km) wide at its narrowest, to finally emerge on the Yamal peninsula.

But the collectivization of the reindeer herds which began in the late 1920s stopped all that. For instance, the biggest reindeer state farm on Yamal, with its 90,000 reindeer, had, like every other state farm, to keep within its own boundaries, so the herds always had to travel through the south of the peninsula irrespective of the depth of snow and could thus lose 60–70 per cent of their number in any one winter. Even after 60-odd years, this still goes on.

In 1978, in one such snowy winter, a Soviet naturalist who happened to be there observed three herds each of about 1500 reindeer which stood up but refused to move despite all the herdsmen's efforts. By the summer they had all been eaten by wolves. For, unlike the wild reindeer, which normally runs away when attacked by wolves, the domesticated reindeer is helpless and when wolves break into a domesticated herd they will kill them all.

The collectivization of the reindeer herds was indeed a tragic absurdity. The Soviet authorities took little account of the reindeers' need to migrate or the reindeer economy, finely tuned over millennia. All herds became state property, to the despair and incomprehension of their nomadic owners, who slaughtered huge numbers of reindeer rather than comply and greatly resisted compulsory settlement in a reindeer farm. As a result of the tundra-wide upheaval and opposition, the domesticated reindeer population fell drastically. In the Koryak National District of Kamchatka, for instance, it dropped by more than half, from 264,000 to 127,000, in the years between 1926 and 1934.

Doubtless wolves played their part in this drama, and reindeer herdsmen must always guard against them, particularly from the onset of darkness in the autumn, when they often attach little bells made from tin cans to the animals' antlers. However, the USSR's most famous predator, *Canis lupus*, the wolf, is found not only in the tundra but in forest, mountain, desert and steppe. A reduction in hunting during the Second World War allowed the wolf population to increase to perhaps 150,000, but for more than ten years up to the late 1950s, an official campaign killed nearly 30,000 a year. In the 1960s and early 1970s hunting pressure eased; wolves were even left alone in some nature reserves, to restore the natural wildlife balance.

The result was a population jump and by 1978 the figure had recovered to some 67,000, particularly in the Altai and other mountain regions of southern Siberia. Since then the number has risen slightly, resulting in increased attacks on livestock and the hunting of wolf packs from aircraft and skidoos, which has now checked the population rise. In 1985 poison was banned, although it is still used in some sparsely populated regions of Siberia. Today a bounty of 150 roubles is paid for one female wolf, 100 for a male and 50 for a cub. But D. I. Bibikov, the leading Soviet wolf expert, has stated that 'Total wolf extermination cannot be justified economically and ecologically.'

It must seem particularly odd to Bibikov that, concurrently with this eradication campaign, wolves are being bred for their fur in state farms in the central regions of Russia. In Alaska and Canada, incidentally, they are also hunted for their fur – the only other parts of the world where they are not in steep decline or reduced to a mere remnant, having already been exterminated in ten European countries, including Britain, France and Germany. As Ewan Clarkson has written in *Wolf Country: A Wilderness Pilgrimage* (Hutchinson, 1976) about North American wolves: 'No war waged by man against another species has been fought so long, or so mercilessly, as has his campaign against the wolf'.

But wolves have an important part to play in the tundra's ecology as predators, both of smaller animals and reindeer. When the reindeer migrate, the wolves follow and have indeed been recorded as following reindeer for

An Arctic fox displays its white winter coat. Arctic fox burrows are normally beneath natural mounds and provide a sheltered habitat for the winter and for rearing young.

90 miles (150 km) and even 120–190 miles (200–300 km). They follow closely to attack exhausted stragglers, and following them come polar foxes and other scavengers – all very useful for the quality control of the herd, as it is the weak and diseased that are killed off.

When the reindeer are not migrating, the wolf stays in its 'home range', within which a permanent network of wolf paths covers the most likely areas for prey. These ranges can be more than 390 square miles (1000 sq km) in area, although in Chukotka, just west of the Bering Strait, one pack of six wolves hunted six domestic reindeer herds within a far greater range of 2900 square miles (7500 sq km) within which it reached a herd every 12–15 days.

Unlike the wolf, the Arctic fox (*Alopex lagopus*) inhabits virtually the entire circumpolar tundra and the Arctic islands of the Soviet Union. Slightly smaller than the European red fox (*Vulpes vulpes*), it is a bold and inquisitive predator, eating birds, eggs, chicks, mice, voles, lemmings and carrion. In rocky coastal areas, where Arctic foxes may feed almost entirely on huge sea-bird colonies, they often make dens in crevices between rocks. But in open, often barren ground they sometimes take over ground squirrel ends or, more usually, dig burrows beneath natural mounds up to 13 ft (4 m) high to allow for both drainage and unfrozen soil above the permafrost. The dens are often easily noticeable because of the rich vegetation, chiefly grasses, around them. This is a result of both the disturbance of the soil during burowing and the humus from the nutritious dung and food remains.

In the summer the Arctic fox's predominantly brown-grey coat fades into the tundra's summer colours all too well for the safety of its prey. In winter its thick, white winter coat – excellent camouflage in the snow – and heavily furred feet and tail make it one of the best insulated of all tundra animals. It can wander astonishingly widely in search of food, not only south into the transitional belt of forest tundra and coniferous forest/taiga beyond, but north on to the ice of the Arctic Ocean. This produces an extraordinary range of sightings, from 50 °N, the latitude of the Mongolian border, to 88 °N, 310 miles (500 km) north to the northernmost Arctic islands.

This departure from terra firma to roam over the sea ice sometimes takes the Arctic foxes hundreds of miles from shore. Their aim, of course, is to find more food on the ice than on land, where winter prey may be restricted to ptarmigan, reindeer carrion and rodents (carcasses of which they find with great skill beneath the snow). On the ice, however, they can predate on sea birds and on ringed seal pups in their lairs, and follow polar bears to scavenge any food left from their kills, mainly of ringed and bearded seals. Carcasses naturally attract them: as many as 40 foxes have been sighted around one dead walrus on the pack ice off Alaska.

In the spring they return to the tundra for the breeding season. As the sea ice breaks up, some find themselves travelling great distances on drifting ice floes and not all of them make it back to land. It is in March, after an almost solitary winter, that the Arctic fox (monogamous until the young are independent) begins to pair, as indicated by double tracks in the snow. It is a

The wolves of Russia range over a wide area which includes the tundra and, in particular, the forests of the taiga where they may hunt elk or reindeer.

Famous for its 'mass suicides', the lemming is a thickly-furred rodent, well adapted to survival in the harsh conditions of the tundra, and feeds mainly on grasses and willow sprigs. Being extensively preyed upon, it is absolutely crucial in the tundra food chain and plays, perhaps, the key role in tundra ecology.

vocal animal, with six different cries, but at this time it gives particularly many calls, which biologists believe are probably those of mated pairs keeping in contact and notifying other foxes of their territory. Litters average around ten cubs but far fewer usually survive, largely because of scarcity of food. The cubs are often born in the open and then carried by their mother to a den where she remains with them for a few days while the male brings in food. Then both parents hunt for food but gradually decrease their care as the cubs grow and expand their little world, until they all disperse around September. And so the cycle of solitary winter ranging begins once more.

The Arctic fox's own predators include wolves, wolverines, polar bears, dogs and red foxes. But man is sometimes the greatest predator, trapping the fox for its pelt – an important economic resource – across the whole circumpolar tundra. Apparently only in the Russian tundra is there any population management, based on numbers obtained from surveying the summer dens. Trapping is then concentrated in the well-populated areas, with each trapper allowed only 150 foxes. The blue-grey pelt of some of the more southerly foxes is highly prized in the international fur trade as 'blue fox', and this animal is still widely bred in Soviet fur farms. Captivity can greatly prolong a fox's life: in the wild, foxes more than five or six years old are rare, while in captivity they have lived up to 14. Incidentally, fur coats may rightly now be anathema in the West, but in the colder parts of the Soviet Union they are by no means luxury items but can be essential for human survival, albeit not necessarily of 'blue fox'.

A growing problem in the Soviet, Canadian and American Arctic (Alaska) is the fox's attraction to man's waste-disposal sites. This is exacerbated by the animals' inquisitive nature and the tundra workers' adoption of individuals as quasi-pets despite their ability to carry rabies, although oddly enough there have been no cases of the disease when humans have been bitten.

A very much smaller prey of the wolf, Arctic fox and other predators, including even the reindeer, is the most famous, and typical, rodent of the tundra: the fat, 5-in (13 cm) long lemming. These busy, thickly furred little creatures almost hug the ground and live in sizeable colonies. Three main species live in the Russian tundra: the Norway lemming (*Lemmus lemmus*) on the Kola peninsula next to the Norway–Finland border and the Siberian and collared lemmings (*Lemmus sibiricus* and *Dicrostonyx torquatus*) in the rest.

Many other tundra animals, including, for instance, the long-tailed suslik (*Citellus parryi*) (close relative of the squirrel) survive the winter in hibernation beneath the snow. The lemmings, by contrast, live busy lives, breeding beneath their snow cover in the space, two to three fingers wide, between ground and snow, made by the earth cooling and emitting steam after falls of snow; where there is no such gap, the lemming burrows through moss. It lines its winter home with a deep layer of dead vegetation and feeds beneath the snow mainly on a mixture of grasses and willow sprigs. The latter it eats to the very roots – the choicest part – supplementing this diet with moss, lichen and fungi.

Nature has provided this tiny rodent with extraordinary powers of procreation beneath the winter's insulatory snow cover, which can raise the temperature of their habitat beneath to some 50 °F (10 °C). The collared lemming has one to three litters annually, but the Siberian lemming has five to six, sometimes one every month from March to September, with an average five or six young per litter: at maximum therefore a 36-fold population jump. Furthermore, at only two or three months the young themselves start to breed, and since the gestation period is only 16–23 days, two or even three generations of lemmings – the earlier ones now reproducing – may be added to the population in a year. This pattern is, of course, dependent on there being enough vegetation to keep the growing numbers alive.

When the melting snow drives them from their cosy homes the newly swollen population must find food for themselves. In a poor year for vegetation, therefore, the population is kept down, if not severely reduced. In a good year, when plant life is plentiful, it explodes. But the tundra

River ice breaking up in the tundra's Taimyr Peninsula as spring approaches.

cannot ultimately provide for anything like all, since each 2-oz (60 gm) lemming eats a lot of vegetation in an average day to fuel its almost relentless activity – a continous pattern of one hour's feeding, two hours' sleeping – throughout the summer's 24-hour daylight. At such population peaks, therefore, the lemming outstrips the food supply, wiping the vegetation from the ground, resorting in desperation to toxic plants and turning aggressive, even to larger animals.

It is then that begin the famous mass migrations in search of food. A whole tide of lemmings rolls across the tundra. Their numbers are reduced *en route* by predators including reindeer and, when they fall into water, by ducks and even fish – but still they come. One leading Soviet tundra biologist, Yuri I. Chernov, has caught 'large specimens of salmon with their stomachs literally stuffed full of lemmings (about ten carcasses in one stomach!)'. And in these 'lemming years', as they are called, the reindeer scarcely fear wolves, for these are gorged on this ample prey which does not even attempt to run away.

As the lemming horde progresses, usually to lower ground, there is only enough food for the few, so it scurries onwards, with so many pressing forward that those in front cannot turn back even when they reach the end of the land. The result is a headlong rush into rivers or seas and mass drowning. The only hope is to swim for it, but almost all perish.

For many centuries these apparent mass suicides were a much-debated mystery. In fact it is more a case of 'manslaughter' by those behind. But it is now known that the excessive number of lemmings is the cause and that the lemming population fluctuates in regular cycles which peak every three to four years. The numbers drop sharply with the 'suicides', and then the cycle starts again.

Just as its supply of food and the weather conditions govern the lemming's dramatic population cycle, so its population size as a food resource dictates to a very great extent the populations of many other tundra species and therefore plays a – even *the* – key role in the tundra's ecology. The numbers of polar fox, ermine, skua, snowy owl, peregrine falcon, rough-legged buzzard and other predatory birds specifically depend on the numbers of lemming, so their populations in turn fluctuate closely with – and as dramatically as – the lemming's cycle. And not only are predators affected but their other prey as well.

In years of low lemming numbers predators are forced to turn their attention elsewhere so that the population of waders, for instance, can decline accordingly. In such years life in the tundra seems almost to stop.

The male and female king eider ducks have markedly different plumage. The female lines the nest with feathers plucked from her breast. It is this nest lining which is highly prized for the manufacture of eiderdowns.

The snowy owl, for instance, which builds its nest near lemming colonies when the population starts to rise, cannot even breed at all; it stays in the same nest for perhaps a year from sheer inertia, catching birds instead, and leaves the area only if the lemming population does not recover the following year. In these trough years many birds and mammals leave the tundra to find food in the taiga, and the Arctic fox must resort to feeding on all the birds it can find beneath the snow. In consequence, the naturalists who are trying to establish nature reserves for tundra birds are now having to regulate the foxes' population. And this whole chain reaction is caused by one little rodent.

In normal years the tundra supports at least 69 species of birds. Among them is the cider (*Somateria mollissima*), which nests almost uninterruptedly along the rocky coasts for some 1180 miles (1900 km) north and south of the Bering Strait. 'Eider down,' a Soviet Arctic biologist has written, 'has been regarded for long as one of the treasures of the North' for its outstandingly good insulating qualities, and the trade in eider down was 'of immense importance in the economy of the Russian North even in the seventeenth century.'

In these stretches of the High Arctic some of the world's biggest bird populations are found in approximately ten sites along the Arctic coast; huge sea-bird colonies (on Wrangel Island of nearly half a million birds). These are the so-called 'bird bazaars' of gulls, auks and cormorants nesting in every crack and on every protrusion of steep rocks and cliff faces. So many birds circle the air that they darken the sky and the endless din of their cries drowns out the crashing waves beneath.

OPPOSITE AND ABOVE *Snowy owl chicks grow very quickly once hatched, feeding solely on lemmings brought to them in the nest by the adult male bird.*

And there are endangered endemic birds here too, among them Ross's roseate gull (*Rhodostethia rosea*), so called from its handsome rosy breast and found (pop. more than 50,000) in only one main area of the eastern Siberian tundra. The magnificent endemic Siberian white crane (*Grus leucogeranus*) nests in almost exactly the same area but with a much lower population of only 2000 at the most, migrating to Iran, India and China in winter. Few birds remain in winter apart from the snowy owl, willow ptarmigan (*Lagopus lagopus*) and rock ptarmigan (*Lagopus mutus*), which, a Soviet ornithologist has discovered, survive the bitter conditions by lowering their body temperatures and thus their essential energy consumption and sheltering in holes beneath the snow, subsisting on an absolute minimum of food. But the rest must migrate, usually thousands of miles, to warmer climes for their survival.

From mid August to early September, for instance, the 135,000-odd Brent geese (*Branta bernicla*) of the western tundra fly west: the dark-bellied subspecies (*B. b. bernicla*) in very large numbers to southern England (particularly East Anglia), the pale-bellied subspecies (*B. b. hrota*) to Denmark, Northumberland and Ireland, while the eastern tundra's 40–60,000, a third subspecies (*B. b. nigricans*), winter mainly in North America.

The 23,000 (maximum) Bewick's swans (*Cygnus columbianus bewickii*) also depart the tundra at this time for Germany, the Netherlands, Britain and Ireland, beginning their long journey home in March. Each bird has a distinct bill pattern and can therefore be recognized individually, so they are God's gift to ornithologists. Every autumn between November and December there is great excitement when the swans arrive at the Wildfowl Trust, founded by Peter Scott at Slimbridge, Gloucestershire, to see if old friends – they all bear names – have returned.

But the winter destinations of the tundra migrants vary enormously. One example is the rare, endemic spoon-billed sandpiper (*Eurynorhynchus pygmeus*), with a population of possibly 2000–2800, although the number is still uncertain. This bird, one of the most elusive and therefore most sought by ornithologists, breeds on the Chukotka peninsula fronting the Bering Strait. However, where it winters was a mystery (other than a few sightings in parts of southern Asia) until as late as 1989 when a flock of 257 was discovered in the Ganges–Brahmaputra delta area of Bangladesh through the international efforts of the Slimbridge-based IWRB Asian Waterfowl Census. This may prove to be the main wintering area, but the bulk of the population is still unaccounted for – perhaps concealed in the unsurveyed part of the delta.

Although very much greater in numbers (around 27,000), the tundra's endemic red-breasted goose (*Branta ruficollis*), is now one of the world's rarest wildfowl. Hunting has reduced it at all stages of its life cycle from perhaps 100,000 or more at the end of the last century. By far the most attractive of all geese with its spectacular black, white and chestnut-red coloration, it breeds only on the Gydansk, Yamal and, above all, Taimyr peninsulas. Arriving at its nesting grounds at the beginning of June, after the other geese – the bean goose (*Anser fabalis*) and the white-fronted goose (*A. albifrous*) – it leaves by the end of August, to winter above all in Romania's

new Danube Delta Biosphere Reserve, although some migrate to Bulgaria, a few to Iran and Azerbaidzan and even north-eastern China, and every two or three years the odd one turns up in Britain.

Almost invariably the red-breasted goose nests near the peregrine falcon (*Falco peregrinus*), which is now restricted to a few thousand pairs in all the tundra and taiga. Odd, seemingly, for a goose to nest near a predator, but the peregrine happens to protect it while protecting her own territory. The peregrine kills birds in flight, seizing only the occasional rodent on the ground, so it is quite harmless to the goose, which walks to nearby water and flies very rarely. The goslings, too, always stroll and do not fly for a long time. But the peregrine chases away polar foxes, snowy owls and other predators. It is actually a defensive alliance, for at the first sign of an intruder the goose takes off, a signal to the peregrine falcon to attack. Yet the male red-breasted goose can be very brave if need be, defending his brood selflessly and even attacking motorboats to allow the female to take her brood out of danger.

Unfortunately, the peregrine falcon's population is only a few thousand pairs, far lower than the red-breasted goose's numbers, and it is declining, partly because of illegal shooting, disturbance and destruction of nests. However, this decline is also due to the disastrous effects 30–40 years ago of pesticides, which today account for a decrease both in fertility and, because of thinning of the egg shells, the number of successful hatchings.

On Wrangel Island, however, north-west of the Bering Strait, there are no peregrines to protect the large snow goose (*Anser caerulescens*) population. These can rely only on the large size of their colonies, where polar foxes dare predate on the periphery alone. Today the snow goose exists in even greater numbers on the Pacific coast of North America, but a century and a half ago it was found for 1000 miles (1600 km) and more right across the Russian tundra between the Lena and the Bering Strait. Since then its numbers have dropped until it has now totally disappeared from the mainland to survive – albeit in massive numbers – only on this island in the Arctic Ocean, uninhabited by man until 1926. There it provided extremely welcome food not only for the settlers but for their sledge dogs as well, and the apparently inexhaustible population began to decline, even though shooting birds to feed the dogs was banned in the early 1930s.

Snow-goose colonies were later made protected areas, with restrictions on shooting and collecting eggs elsewhere on the island. Nonetheless the population fell by more than half in only six years: from some 120,000 in 1970 to only 50,000 in 1976. A major reason was the habitat's disruption by the introduction of domesticated reindeer. As their numbers grew, some of the reindeer became wild and invaded the geese's nesting grounds to eat their eggs. Moreover, dead reindeer sustained the geese's chief enemy, the Arctic fox, whose population therefore multiplied rapidly. The result was that so many eggs and chicks perished that the surviving young could not possibly compensate for the adult mortality.

With the snow goose's population falling so fast, a state nature reserve (*zapovednik*) was established on Wrangel Island in 1976, the reindeer population was reduced and a joint US–USSR conservation programme set up to establish the behaviour and migratory routes of this bird which the two nations had in common. More than a thousand snow geese were fitted with orange-coloured collars to distinguish them from the North American geese, which are regarded as game birds, and the chief ornithologists involved, William Sladen and Alexander Alexandrovich Kishchinsky, were able to compile a great deal of hitherto unknown data about this beautiful goose. As a result, the USA and Canada imposed specific hunting restrictions, and by the early 1980s the Soviet population had doubled to nearly 100,000 and by 1989 was approaching 200,000, well above the target of 120,000 set in the US–USSR agreement.

The Wrangel Island nature reserve was set up to protect not only the snow goose but the world's largest breeding grounds of the Pacific walrus (*Odeobenus rosmarus-divergens*) as well as the greatest number of polar bear dens in the Soviet Arctic. Sometimes there are more than 80,000 walruses massed on the capes and spits of the island in the breeding season between mid-July and November. So tightly packed are they that when one of the massive beasts plunges into the sea, another one promptly takes its place. Many arguments result from the congestion and are often solved with the ivory tusks (carved by the indigenous peoples) which project about 18 in (46 cm) beyond the jaw in the case of the male (although these are much shorter in the female).

These are the largest pinnipeds of the northern hemisphere, up to 13 ft (4 m) in length and more than a ton in weight. They feed largely on the soft part of molluscs, crushing the shells with teeth which have evolved specially to do so. In the past, man exterminated many walruses for the tough leather produced from their skin and for the oil extracted from their blubber. In recent years, however, their population has risen substantially thanks to an international programme for their conservation. Both the walrus and polar bear programmes represent successes for international conservation (just as the snow goose is an excellent example of bilateral nature protection). In 1965 the USSR and the other five Arctic nations agreed to an exchange of scientific data on the polar bear and to a sharp curb on hunting, which became a total ban in 1973. (A small quota is allowed for some northern peoples, but in the USSR the prohibition is total.) As a result the world's polar-bear population has, at the very least, doubled in only 20–25 years, rising from 8–10,000 in 1965–70 to 20–40,000 in 1990. And in the Soviet Arctic there are now some 5–7,000.

But Wrangel Island is only one of five nature reserves in the tundra. The first to be established, in 1939, was Kandalaksha on the Kola peninsula, which has had various sections added to it over the years. Since 1975 it has formed part of a White Sea bay area which has been declared a wetland of international importance. On the same peninsula is also the Lapland Reserve, and on the Taimyr peninsula (as of 1979) the great Taimyr Reserve of more than 5000 square miles (13,483 sq km), the second largest in the USSR, after the Ust–Lensky Reserve of 5530 square miles (14,330 sq km) further east in the Lena delta.

Such reserves are greatly to be welcomed, for the tundra is the most delicate of all the earth's ecosystems. This northern ecosystem is extremely vulnerable to any man-made impact. It can take years for the vegetation to recover from the passage of one human being, let alone one vehicle. Even the age-old reindeer husbandry itself can be harmful, for continuous grazing has already encouraged erosion, forming bogs and even lakes. According to Soviet experts, the Yamal peninsula can sustain 26,000 reindeer but has nearly 44,000 (the majority in private herds), so each year many acres of pasture are lost from overgrazing, and reindeer moss takes more than 50 years to grow 3 in (8 cm).

However, the impact of industrial development is infinitely greater than that of overgrazing. It is the exploration and extraction of the tundra's mineral wealth which takes the heaviest toll. Motor vehicles, caterpillar tracks, construction equipment, air and water pollution and so on play havoc with this ultra-sensitive ecosystem. Under the onslaught vegetation is destroyed (sometimes the Iceland moss and tundra peatbogs are burnt accidentally) and like a stack of cards the whole system collapses. With the vegetation gone, the permafrost beneath starts to thaw, intensive thermo-karst processes begin, any slopes become eroded – after the loss of vegetation from even only a small part – bogs and lakes form, wildlife declines and changes, and even the microclimate alters.

Some of the tundra's environmental problems are not of its own making. Economic activity in the taiga to the south has brought the migration of pesticides and other toxic compounds which have affected its wildlife populations – although it is the use of insecticides against the tundra's gadflies and other voracious insects which has resulted in findings of DDT residues in lemmings and birds. In the south, too, 100,000 ton of oil are estimated to leak into western Siberia's river system each year, largely from the oil industry's decaying retention ponds set in the vast plain's wetlands. Some of it sinks, but some makes its way to the tundra.

Unfortunately oil pollution as well as the burning off of natural gas and mineral extraction, particularly destabilizes the tundra ecosystem because of the painfully slow breakdown rate of pollutants here and their destructive effect on moss, especially the reindeer's winter pastures. Coastal waters too are polluted, particularly by oil and oil products, greatly reducing the number of sea birds.

Not only have lakes and rivers become polluted but the very air as well. Acid rain now falls on the entire tundra except the Yamal peninsula and the extreme north-east. One major culprit is the Norilsk smelting complex, which emits each year an estimated 2.5 million tonnes of sulphur dioxide alone, much the same quantity as that emitted by the whole of Canada, and is almost certainly a substantial contributor to Arctic haze and pollution of the Arctic Ocean via the River Yenisei.

Fortunately intensive extraction is confined to a relatively small proportion of the tundra. But two peninsulas of north-western Siberia are undergoing huge natural-gas development projects with major environmental impacts. Yamburg, on the Taz peninsula, is the site of the world's second largest gas deposit (the largest, Urengoi, is a mere 170 miles/275 km south-east) and here a line of drilling rigs and their infrastructure now rises above the tundra.

On the Yamal, the next peninsula west, the almost equally rich gas fields have brought innumerable exploratory shafts, a mass of abandoned machinery, pollution from the drill lubricants and the destruction of enormous tracts of tundra, not least by huge earth-moving vehicles. So far about 2500 square miles (6470 sq km) of reindeer pasture have been lost. In 1986 construction was begun here of the world's northernmost railway line, to extend 310 miles (500 km) due north up the peninsula. The objective was both to transport up to 9 million tonnes of freight a year and to carry the machinery with which to build ten parallel pipelines to take the gas south and on to Europe. The projected result is a swath of disturbance 1¼ miles (2 km) wide across the reindeer migration routes. Abandoned quarries for the foundations and the flooded tracks left by dump trucks now scar the area, and the half-built railway line undulates dangerously owing to the instability of the permafrost below.

However, as a result of the protests of environmentalists and the local Nentsy (who have herded reindeer on the Yamal since the second century BC) as well as the influence of the media, work on the railway and pipeline has been suspended while less damaging routes are investigated. But the USSR's rapidly deteriorating economy badly needs this natural wealth, and at present oil and gas exports earn 80 percent of the nation's crucial hard currency. In the circumstances the economy seems very likely to win over the environment, although the head of the Institute for Problems of the North, Vladimir Melnikov, warned in 1988 that 'if one sticks to the old approach – gas and oil at any cost – then the Arctic tundra will be in for an ecological catastrophe'. Five years earlier a leading tundra biologist, V. A. Zabrodin, had stated ominously that 'The fundamental, often irreversible, reformation of the entire ecosystem is taking place.'

Yet it is not only the ecosystem that is suffering. Man is his own victim too, although those who suffer here have had no control over their plight. In Norilsk, for instance, there is a high incidence of respiratory disease and other pollution-related illnesses. But the most serious long-term problem for both man and the environment is the legacy of the nuclear tests of the 1950s and 1960 in the far north. In Chukotka, the extreme north-eastern region facing Alaska, the ecology now suffers a high level of radioactivity, and the population's average dose of radiation is approximately the same as that received by the population around Chernobyl. What is more, the Chukchi reindeer people's dose is worsened by the simple food chain which ends with them: from lichen to reindeer to man.

The result for the Chukchi is grave health problems including an incidence of liver cancer ten times higher than average, a doubling of leukaemia and stomach tumours and tripling of lung cancer in the last 20 years, and the world's highest rate for cancer of the oesophagus. Almost 100 percent of the native population suffer from tuberculosis and 90 percent from chronic lung disease. The life expectancy of the Chukchi people (excluding accidents) is now only 45 years. In the six years up to 1989 infant mortality rose by 6 percent to a rate of between 70 and 100 births per 1000.

Meanwhile, the Nentsy reindeer breeders of Novaya Zemlya, the large Arctic island at the other end of Siberia, protested in a 1989 petition to the Supreme Soviet that 33 years of nuclear tests – at least 121 underground and atmospheric tests have taken place – had brought abnormally high cancer rates, since the lichens and berries which the reindeer eat are excessively high in radioactive isotopes. The Soviet government, however, announced that Kazakhstan, far to the south, was being abandoned as a nuclear testing ground and that all future nuclear tests would be held on Novaya Zemlya. A Novaya Zemlya–Nevada Committee was set up to fight the latter decision, and Greenpeace, the international environmental movement, attempted (unsuccessfully) to land protesters on the island, but in October 1990 a test took place.

To revert to the chief foundation of tundra society: the reindeer. In the past 20 years more than 77,000 square miles (200,000 sq km) of reindeer pasture has been destroyed – almost the size of England and Scotland combined. Some 23,000 square miles (60,000 sq km) of this has been lost in the (theoretically) autonomous Nentsy area alone which embraces the Yamal and Taz peninsulas, scene of so much gas-related activity. And the total figure does not include the land which will regenerate to reindeer pasture in half a century provided it is not grazed meanwhile. As a result the reindeer population has dropped in the last 30 years from 2.4 million in 1965 to 1.8 million in 1986. And since the way of life of most of these indigenous peoples is founded on the reindeer herds, they are lost without them. With no alternative livelihood, their very existence both collectively and individually is now being threatened.

In the free and more democratic society now emerging in the USSR, more and more of them are finding their voice to complain bitterly that their land, their wildlife and their traditional way of life are being ruined. It is indeed a human and environmental tragedy.

Where has the pristine tundra gone? It is the old story of man the predator, his irresponsibility and his use of new destructive technologies, compounded here by the constraints of the Soviet state system. And here in the most delicate ecosystem on earth, the consequences are unfortunately the longest-lasting. But the Russians and other peoples of the USSR are increasingly concerned, if not angry, about their environment as the true picture emerges under glasnost.

Hopefully, given time, the relationship between man and nature will radically improve in all this vast country's different ecosystems. Of these, by far the biggest, many times the size of the tundra and providing an almost total contrast to its treeless expanse, is the greatest forest on earth: the taiga.

Richard Kemp, cameraman on the Taimyr peninsula, the northernmost point of Eurasia

After almost a week of high winds and heavy snowfall we emerged one morning to find the sombre grey skies had changed to a pastel blue, and wispy clouds were scudding over the nearby hills. To complete the scene and etch it indelibly into my memory, a small herd of eight stag reindeer moved lazily across the skyline, their great antlers swaying to and fro as they moved. They stopped from time to time to excavate a patch of snow, digging deep to forage on the moss and lichen that lay hidden below. When the snow lies thick the deer may have to dig so deep that only the tips of their tails are visible above the snow, but here the wind had scoured it away from the tops, leaving scanty grasses and dwarf birch near the surface. They were the first to reach Pura that season. More isolated groups were to pass through, followed by the females that were ready to drop their calves, but we were not to see the really big migrating herds until mid July.

The ice on the rivers was terribly thick – 10 ft (3 m) or so. It breaks up quickly in June in a couple of days with a terrific clanging and banging. It's already softish and scrunches when it runs into the pack ice at a bend. The ice tinkles when it falls off, but from a distance you just hear a continuous grinding, swishing noise. The main break up came around 2 am. We heard the noise and found later that the ice we'd been walking across all day had disappeared. Mini-icebergs rushed by and we could feel the ice sheet we were standing on moving below us. I was filming one mini-iceberg approaching about 1 ft (30 cm) above water. Then it struck the ice ahead and reared up out of the water, the size of a hut. I hadn't bargained for its size, but luckily our Russian interpreter pulled me out of the way, otherwise I'd have been knocked flat at the very least.

Barbara Maas, assistant to David Shale, cameraman on Wrangel Island in the Arctic Ocean

Standing as still as possible, the very tip of my nose being the only part of my body exposed to the roaring wind, I waited for the foxes. I didn't immediately realize that the small white blob

which had emerged in one of the barely visible entrance holes of the den was the head of an Arctic fox. There we were, looking at each other, him with alert and inquisitive black eyes and me a huge red and blue monstrosity afraid to make the slightest movement lest I should frighten him. I rapidly began to feel intensely uncomfortable and noticed that I had in fact stopped breathing. Moments later the whole fox appeared, scent-marked a spot next to his den and without wasting another glance at me trotted off into the tundra. When I got back to my room that day I found that the end of my nose had gone white. Two days later the skin began to peel off. The new skin which followed grew a dark brown colour and remained a permanent feature of my face for months.

After that first day I spent about three or four hours every day in front of the fox den. Squatting on two reindeer skins, I observed and photographed the resident Arctic foxes. At least five foxes, three males and two females, seemed to be leading a more or less peaceful coexistence in this den. Since it was close to the place where the islanders carry out their annual reindeer culls, food was no problem. I was able to observe the comings and goings of the foxes, their play and their squabbling, in which two of the males in particular were intermittently engaged. With a humorous stealthy gait, bushy white tails erect, they chased each other around the den and up onto the precarious roof of the wooden shed, where they would interrupt their engagement for a brief moment to scan the surroundings before flying down again onto the icy snow. There they would eventually separate and, facing each other from a safe distance, would bark into the silent air, each of them sending up a small white cloud.

CHAPTER THREE

THE ENDLESS FOREST

'Everything [in the Barguzin taiga reserve on the east coast of Lake Baikal] has remained as it was many centuries ago, when humans first set foot here. Twilight and tranquility always reign in the dense taiga, under the thick branches of cedar, fir, and spruce fir trees. There are no bushes, no wild grass. Around are only mosses, lichens, mushrooms and, rarely, ferns, and *Bergenia*. Sharing space with fallen moss-covered giant trees are fantastically interlaced roots. Branches freshly broken by storms intertwine with dry twigs covered by grey lichens. Working one's way through this chaos of wind-fallen wood, twigs and branches is extremely difficult. The legs stumble against roots concealed in moss, slip over moist stones and land in prehensile dry twigs and branches, which stick out here and there, prick the face, scratch the hands and tear clothes. Soaring in the air are countless swarms of mosquitoes and midges . . .

You raise your head and see only a scrap of sky between the tops of the giant trees. The impression is as though one is at the bottom of a woody canyon separated from the outer world by an endless high-trunk tree taiga. The solemn silence is only occasionally interrupted by the shrill cries of nutcrackers (*Nucifraga caryocatactes*) and the hollow drumming knocks of woodpeckers. Singing birds are quite rare in the dark coniferous taiga – only titmice and chiffchaffs chirp at the very tops of trees. They never fly down . . .

Though quiet, the dense taiga reserve is full of life. Inquisitive faces of squirrels peep from behind cedar trunks; ubiquitous striped Siberian chipmunks flash among roots; at dusk the large-eyed flying squirrel

Autumn is the most beautiful time in the taiga with a magnificent range of brown, yellow, orange and gold set against the deep green of pines and firs.

Pteromys volans noiselessly glides down on the adjacent tree. But the dark coniferous . . . taiga is primarily the kingdom of sables.'
(Vladimir Kozhevoi in M. Davydova and V. Kozhevoi's *Nature Reserves in the USSR*, Progress Publishers, Moscow, 1989)

An enormous coniferous forest, more than twice the size of the Amazon rainforest, stretches 4000 miles (6400 km) across the northern USSR – from the Finnish border to the Pacific. This is the taiga, the largest forest in the world, and by far the Soviet Union's largest habitat: a 1500-mile (2500 km) wide belt across the entire country, between the tundra to the north and the steppe to the south, and almost unbroken except for the patchwork effect in the western Siberian wetlands. To the south of these lie great forests predominantly of birch, which gave rise to the nineteenth-century euphemism for those exiled to Siberia: 'sent to count the birches'. Mixed deciduous and coniferous forests are confined to very disjointed sections in European Russia, after centuries of felling and land clearing, as well as to the very south of the Soviet Far East (see Chapter 8).

Anyone who flies for hour after hour across the taiga's vast expanse, dark green from horizon to horizon, can hardly fail to be impressed by its vastness. It is called alternatively the boreal – that is, northern – forest after Boreas, the god of the north wind in ancient Greek mythology. A very similar, although much smaller, forest is found in North America's comparable latitudes, and this is also sometimes referred to as taiga. Most of the mosses and lichens, important components of the forest, are the same in both and each forest is composed of pines, larches, spruces and firs. But the tree species are different, and the USSR's Scots pine (*Pinus sylvestris*) is replaced by the Jack pine (*Pinus banksia*) in North America and each tree species of the taiga has a corresponding yet somewhat differing species in the North American forest. The same is largely true for the flowering plants, such as the lovely May lily (*Maianthemum bifolium*) found across much of Europe and Asia, but most abundant in the taiga, and replaced in the North American forest by the wild lily of the valley.

All this may have puzzled early naturalists, but it is now thought that the world's coniferous forests first developed in mountainous areas of warmer regions more than 50 million years ago. This was followed by a gradual cooling of the global climate, which allowed these early forests to spread into the lowlands. At times of low sea level, when the land bridge of Beringia, connecting Eurasia with North America, was exposed, the two great forests sometimes merged, and both animals and plants crossed from one to the other. Over the ensuing millennia the differences between the species have slowly evolved.

Vast the taiga may be and uniform at first sight, but only to the uninitiated. In the first place, it alters from north to south. In a transitional zone with the tundra, hardy dwarf birch, alder and willow increasingly occupy sheltered pockets, and further south they gradually coalesce, low-growing conifers appear and tundra vegetation is confined to the most exposed areas. When the trees become dominant the taiga begins.

It is, however, in this transitional zone of wooded tundra that many of the tundra's animals give way to the animals of the taiga. The long-furred

Arctic fox (*Alopex lagopus*), for instance, blue-grey to white in colour, becomes less abundant and the shorter furred red fox (*Vulpes vulpes*) more common. Reindeer (*Rangifer tarandus*) diminish, although they are still to be found, and the elk (*Alces alces*), with its longer legs adapted to the deep forest snow, increases. The grazing geese and wading sandpipers, stints and phalaropes of the tundra ecology start to be replaced by the thrushes, tits and warblers and other birds of the taiga, dependent on its insects, nuts and berries.

In this northern, open, conifer woodland with its understorey of lichens and shrubs, the winter wind prevents the accumulation of deep snow and it is then that the region becomes the domain of the wolf (*Canis lupus*). Although it ranges from tundra to steppe, it can move at deadly speed over the shallower compacted snow; the wolf's optimum winter hunting ground is here, where it pursues the elk and reindeer, its preferred prey. In winter

The red fox hunts mainly at night, although the vixen will also catch prey during the day when there are cubs to be fed.

A tiny section of the vast uninhabited taiga.

the normally solitary elks band together to form small herds, making themselves an easier target for the wolf packs, which bring down the young, weak and old. Yet instinct compels them to herd together in winter because, on balance, there is a better chance of survival. Helpfully for the wolf too, the severe winter leads many reindeer to take shelter in the taiga, where they feed on reindeer moss (*Cladonia rangiferina*).

Further south the forest becomes increasingly dense and in places is carpeted in deep moss with a few shrubs and flowering plants beneath the thick canopy. But it is an enormous mosaic of the taiga's different habitats, varying sometimes within only a few hundred yards. The gentle sound of the wind stirring the treetops may be interrupted by the occasional bird call or the roar of a bull elk, but usually the taiga is silent. This region, the true taiga, extends south for hundreds of miles and is the realm of many animals, including the great brown bear (*Ursus arctos*), lynx (*Felis lynx*), sable (*Martes zibellina*) and a profusion of birds and rodents.

From west to east the tree cover of the taiga varies dramatically. Spruce dominates to the Urals, then chiefly pine, spruce and fir to the River Yenisei, while immediately to the east larches, particularly the Daurian larch (*Larix dahurica*), reign supreme right to the Sea of Okhotsk.

The reason for the abrupt change – and of animals too – lies in the difference of climate on either side of the Yenisei, the boundary between the great western plain and the equally expansive Central Siberian Plateau. West of the river, the climate is somewhat moderated by the warm, wet weather systems due, even here, to the Atlantic. But east, above the plateau, the belt of high pressure lasting most of winter prevents the moderating air masses from reaching the area. Winter may be cold enough in the west, but temperatures east of the Yenisei can plunge to around −94 °F (−70 °C). The notorious Siberian winter has led to an impression of permanent cold – perhaps even perpetual snow – but this is to ignore the hot, albeit short, summers, which can register over 95 °F (35 °C). Snow cover itself is in fact not usually deep, with overall snow and rainfall in the west at around 20 in (50 cm) – slightly lower than London's and less than half New York's – and the east is much drier, with some areas drier than Australia's Alice Springs.

It is these different climates which determine the tree composition of the taiga. West of the Yenisei the trees have to cope with modest precipitation, long, cold winters with fairly heavy snowfall and short summers. The region's evergreen conifers are ideally suited to this, for their needles are designed for minimum water loss and their waxy coating provides effective protection from frost. Their Christmas tree shape, being evolved to prevent damage from heavy snowfalls, helps them survive the long, hard winter and retain their needles so that they are ready to exploit the short summer sun to the full.

The larches are adapted to even harsher conditions, but are deciduous, shedding their leaves in winter to prevent any water loss or what would be certain damage from the severe temperatures. Moreover, the predominant Daurian larch has shallow spreading roots, perfect for capturing precious water, where permafrost traps it in the upper layers of the soil. So larch dominates an enormous area where few other trees can survive.

The lakes of the taiga gradually fill in owing to the mud deposited by inflowing streams and the accumulation of dead reeds and other plants, which together form a peaty sediment. This slowly fills the lake basin, turning it into a swamp, and then rotting plants raise its surface above the level of the water-table, forming drier patches which can then be colonized by shrubs or trees.

Some processes, however, stop lakes and wetlands from drying out. One role in this is played by the beaver – *Castor fiber* in Eurasia and in North America *C. canadensis*, only marginally different – the largest rodent of Europe and Asia, sometimes exceeding 5 ft (1.5 m) in length including its 1-ft (30 cm) paddle-shaped tail. Beavers build their dams in order to provide lodges in which they can live as pairs with one or two litters. The lodges are well insulated, especially when covered with snow, and have underwater entrances which allow the beavers to remain active through the winter, feeding off bundles of twigs stored beneath the pond's frozen surface and safe from the hungriest of predators.

THIS PAGE AND OPPOSITE *Once close to extinction owing to the popularity of its fur, the beaver has been reintroduced success- fully in many areas and its population has greatly increased. It feeds almost exclusively on bark gnawed from the trunks and branches of trees.*

Unwittingly, the beaver creates a complex wetland environment suitable for fish and water birds, with surrounding meadows providing valuable grazing for forest herbivores. In addition the dammed river raises the local water-table, increasing moisture in the soil and thus promoting more vigorous tree growth.

Beavers have been hunted for their fur in what is now the USSR since at least the seventh or eighth century. Archaeologists have found numerous iron and bone arrowheads with their points blunted to avoid damaging the animals' pelts. Despite this historic depredation, Philip Strahlenberg, a captured Swedish officer, could write in the mid eighteenth century in the first serious study of Siberia that they were still 'in great Abundance . . . and very cheap' in several parts of Siberia despite still being hunted, and he commented that the Russians and Tatars distinguished 'two different Species . . . *those that are idle* and . . . *those that work*; The latter have the worst Skins, because they do much labour in gathering their Provisions for the Winter . . . those who are idle are more liable to be hunted, because of their fine Skins, and the others, because they feed those, are the more spar'd; From which, a very apt Application might be made to Human Life.'

By the early twentieth century the beaver was almost extinct, down to under 1000, but since then it has been successfully reintroduced in many river systems of European Russia and reacclimatized, particularly in the Voronezh and Berezina reserves. In some remoter areas it has been reportedly dropped in by parachute in special cages which open on impact. Its population has increased many tens of times and it is nowadays once more hunted for its fur.

The beaver copes with the Siberian winter by profoundly modifying its environment, but in these low temperatures certain predators, such as the wolverine (*Gulo gulo*), remain active, hunting weakened prey. However, herbivores such as the elk must either change their diet, consuming what is available, or, like the red squirrel (*Sciurus vulgaris*) and Siberian chipmunk (*Eutamias sibiricus*) – two of the taiga's most abundant rodents – rely on large food stores accumulated in the autumn. Other animals, especially birds, migrate to escape the winter entirely, risking long, frequently hazardous journeys every year.

Predators such as the brown bear hibernate, living off stored body fats, while the predators of the Mustelid family, such as the sable, stoat, pine marten and Siberian weasel, remain active, their tracks evident in the snow. The largest member of this family, and found also in the North American taiga, is the wolverine. It is about 18 in (45 cm) at the shoulder and up to 39 in (100 cm) long to the end of its bushy tail and weighs up to 66 lb (30 kg). It tends to live in swampier areas, which its closest rival, the wolf, prefers to avoid. Although the wolverine is a match for a single wolf, when confronted with a pack it has to seek the safety of the trees and it is this factor above all which prevents it venturing onto the treeless tundra (except where hunters have reduced the wolf population).

As its alternative name, the glutton, might imply, the animal is not generally well loved and indeed is reputed for its ferocity, although one Swedish naturalist who hand-reared four wolverine cubs found them loyal and affectionate long after their release. But it is a misleading nickname, for the wolverine does not have a voracious appetite. However, it is omnivorous, its summer diet embracing wasp larvae, berries, eggs and the occasional deer or elk, although it makes little attempt at stealth and has scant success with quicker-footed animals in summer. In winter, however, its prowess as a hunter is fully realized. With the snow cover its approach can be silent and its broad paws make it surefooted and faster than its prey, turning it into a deadly predator, even of the lynx. With its thick fur, it needs only take to its den in the heaviest snowstorm, while during fair weather it can remain active for a full 24 hours, covering as much as 40 miles (65 km) in that time.

The most famous of the taiga's mustelids is the handsome sable (*Martes zibellina*), considerably smaller than the wolverine at less than 2 ft (60 cm) long, including a 6-in (15 cm) tail, and weighing only 3–4 lb (1.5–2 kg). Similarly active through the winter, the sable is a fiercely territorial animal, often eliminating all weasels and stoats from its range, from which it strays only in times of severe food shortage. It is now found only in the more isolated areas of the taiga east of the River Pechora, owing to its centuries-long persecution, but its numbers have risen immeasurably over the past decades, and it is protected above all in the Barguzin reserve.

Frequently nesting in hollows in trees or in rock crevices, it survives the winter's absence of nuts and berries by plunging beneath the snow after small mammals such as the northern red-backed vole (*Clethrionomys rutilus*) and the wood lemming (*Myopus schisticolor*). In early spring the male is very attentive to the female, bearing her gifts of food. This was thought to be part of a prenuptial courtship, but when attempts at captive breeding continually failed it was realized that, unlike most of its relatives, the sable mates in midsummer and not in early spring as had been thought previously. When the embryos are partially developed their growth actually stops until spring. The male's attention in spring is not merely part of courtship but for the sake of the imminent litter. The whole process gives the young sable a head-start in the taiga's short summer.

The 'master of the taiga', the subject of endless folklore and a boon to Western writers and cartoonists as Russia's national emblem, is the

The wolverine is a ferocious predator, said to fear only man. Extremely powerful, it is capable of bringing down prey as large as reindeer.

Female brown bears have litters of up to three cubs which are born in a den, cave or natural snow-covered hollow in the ground. The cubs normally stay with their mothers for two years before becoming independent.

European brown bear (*Ursus arctos*). In winter, unlike the busy sable and wolverine, it remains virtually inactive, in a state of semi-hibernation. At other seasons it may have several, usually simple, dens with little apparent thought of comfort, but the winter den is chosen with much greater care as it will be home for six months and must be dry, well insulated, secure and comfortable.

For preference the bear will take up residence in a cave, carefully blocking the entrance with leaves and branches. In some cases it uses leaves to fill in any hollows in the cave floors. In the absence of a cave, the bear either digs a deep den in the ground or settles for a natural depression next to a tree in order to be beneath an insulating layer of snow. Only a small breathing hole is left open, through which appears a tell-tale vapour. The female gives birth to a litter of up to three cubs in mid to late winter, so she is especially careful about selecting a den, which must double as a nursery.

The brown bear is an intimidating animal, particularly in eastern Siberia, where it stands more than 10 ft (3 m) tall when on its hind legs and weighs up to three quarters of a ton (760 kg) – as much as ten average men. In order to support this great bulk through winter without food it must eat heavily in late summer and autumn, consuming a wide variety of energy-rich food, such as berries, fungi, insects, earthworms, fish, deer and elk. In this manner it puts on enough weight to maintain its body temperature at a slightly reduced 95 °F (35 °C) throughout the winter, lowering its daily consumption of calories to roughly that of an active human, and not truly hibernating but merely dozing with a slowed heart rate. If disturbed it becomes immediately alert and may even leave the comfort of its lair on warmer days. Even more remarkable is the mother's ability to sustain both herself and her new-born cubs on her fat stores. The cubs are tiny when born, weighing less than 1 lb (0.5 kg) – only about the same size as a red squirrel. Their size allows the semi-hibernating mother an easy birth and avoids excessive suckling demands. The female can breed every other year and is very occasionally accompanied by two generations of cubs, each of which hibernates with her through one or, in some cases, two winters, waiting until their third year before braving the winter alone.

Not all animals of the taiga cope as well as the brown bear with the sub zero temperatures. For some, particularly the herbivores, it can be a time of great hardship. The taiga's largest herbivore is the elk (*Alces alces*), which in summer grazes in the meadows and among the water plants of ponds and shallow lakes. As these are quickly unattainable with the arrival of frost and snow, it forms small groups which feed on the bark and foliage of the trees. The world's largest deer, standing up to 7 ft (2.1 m) tall at the shoulder, and weighing as much as a brown bear, the elk consumes great quantities of vegetation – around 4 tons in the winter alone – causing considerable damage to the taiga. Despite its very long legs it finds movement easier in the shallower snow but generally leaves an area only when food becomes scarce, using existing tracks to reduce the risk of attracting wolves. The small herds split up in spring: females bear their young alone and most of the others return to the abundant food sources of the marshes and riverside meadows.

No animal with the appetite of the elk would find it possible to store enough food to last the winter months. But many of the taiga's smaller residents survive in this way, such as the squirrel and the nutcracker (*Nucifraga caryocatactes*), both of which spend much of their time in autumn gathering and storing nuts.

A member of the crow family found throughout the taiga, the nutcracker is easily identified by its deep-brown plumage covered in white spots. The Siberian race (*N. c. macrorhynchos*) has a thinner bill than its European relative (*N. c. caryocatactes*) and, despite its name, feeds mostly on pine seeds. This intriguing bird, rather than remove seeds individually with its long, slender bill, dashes whole pine cones against a tree or the ground in order to shake free the seeds. In autumn it gathers large numbers of them in a special pouch under its tongue and flies off to secrete its cargo in soft soil or piles of moss, or beneath the bark of a tree. Prudently it spreads the seeds between a number of different places, remembering all their positions even when they are hidden by snow.

After a good harvest of pine seeds the nutcracker has no difficulty surviving the winter, even though it may have to burrow through snow to reach the hoarded seeds, and the new year's population will consequently be high. But if the next harvest is poor the increased population soon runs out of food and is forced to search for it elsewhere. This sequence occurred in

A nutcracker eating seeds. This crow-like bird will also scavenge for meat although its usual diet is more likely to include fruit, seeds, nuts and invertebrate animals.

the poor cone year of 1968 which, coinciding with an early snowfall, precipitated a mass exodus of nutcrackers from the Siberian taiga. Exceptionally, several hundred of them reached Britain and France, much to the delight of the bird-watchers of both countries. But, because nutcrackers rarely adapt well to a new environment, many meet an early demise, and these spasmodic emigrations are sometimes called 'death-wanderings'.

Other birds of the taiga such as the crossbills (for instance, *Loxia leucoptera*) undergo similar fluctuations in numbers. Some species, however, manage to survive without emigrating: members of the grouse family, for instance – the most common birds of the taiga – which spend the full year in the forest. Among these are the northern hazel grouse (*Bonasa bonasia*), the western capercaillie (*Tetrao urogallus*) and the black-billed capercaillie (*T. parvirostris*).

The capercaillies are splendid birds, weighing up to 14 lb (6 kg), with dark glossy plumage and, in the male, white undersides to their tails. Almost exclusively vegetarian, as small chicks they eat only insects, turning as adults to berries, flowers and fruit in summer and in winter to pine shoots and needles, digestible thanks to certain micro-organisms in their intestines. On fair winter days they remain in the trees for long periods, but when the

A female western capercaillie and chick. The nest is usually built at the foot of a tree or beside a fallen branch, well camouflaged amongst the vegetation of the forest.

weather worsens they shelter in holes in the snow. The black-billed capercaillie, however, mostly of the eastern taiga, is prevented by a lower snowfall from taking refuge in such snow holes, and remains in the trees, sheltering both from the elements and predators such as owls and hawks.

The hazel grouse shares many of the capercaillie's habits, such as its diet, use of snow holes and very large crop (a pouch-shaped enlargement of the gullet). The latter allows the bird, active for only short periods during the brief winter days, to eat large quantities of food which can then be digested slowly through the long night, and it also warms the frozen fodder on its way to the stomach. In the mountainous areas of eastern Siberia the hazel grouse migrates up the mountains to areas of deeper snow, presumably to enable it to construct its snow hole. To its misfortune, it is much prized for its flesh and although spring may bring an abundance of food it brings the hunters too.

For most of the birds of the taiga winter is too severe to tolerate and an enormous variety of birds, including swans, ducks, thrushes and warblers, leave the taiga every autumn to risk long and often arduous migrations, returning again in spring. One of the smallest migrants is the Siberian accentor (*Prunella montanella*), the same size as its cousin, the dunnock,

A drake goldeneye, capable of diving to great depths to feed on aquatic worms and small crustaceans.

and endemic to the eastern Siberian taiga. Rather shy and with a louder song than the dunnock, in winter it migrates eastwards as far as China and Korea – no mean feat for a bird of its size. Smaller still are the willow warbler (*Phylloscopus trochilus*) and chiffchaff (*P. collybita*) which breed in the taiga, feeding on the summer swarms of flying insects, and in winter migrate several thousand miles to Africa.

Two attractively coloured ducks are the goosander (*Mergus merganser*) and the goldeneye (*Bucephala clangula*). The goosander drake has a dark-green head and long, red bill, the female a chestnut-coloured head with a white chin. Both dive beneath the surface of lakes, rivers and even fast-flowing streams, using their long, saw-edged bills to catch fish such as eels and salmon. The goldeneye – the head is dark green in the drake and chocolate brown in the female – is also a diving duck, sometimes to a depth of 30 ft (9 m), but its diet is based more on aquatic worms, molluscs, small crustaceans and insects than on fish.

What makes both species of duck exceptional is that they nest in holes in trees, usually those abandoned by the black woodpecker (*Dryocopus martius*). These are normally more than 8 ft (2.5 m) but sometimes up to 16 ft (5 m) off the ground in the case of the goldeneye and up to 60 ft (18 m) in the case of the goosander. As a consequence the chicks have to jump from a considerable height just after hatching, well before they can fly.

The return of migrating birds to the taiga from west, east and south signifies the onset of spring. As the snow melts and the ice-bound rivers start to flow with increasing speed, producing floods, the taiga's winter beauty of white and grey turns to the rich greens and browns of summer. Fresh green shoots push through the carpets of coniferous needles, fungi sprout from dormant spores and the trees soak up the welcome sunlight of the lengthening days. When the thaw is complete and winter is banished, it is another world.

Early in spring the female bear, hungry after the long semi-hibernation, leaves her lair and cubs to find food, and as the weather warms, the cubs, now the size of small dogs, venture out with her. Playful and inquisitive in their new environment, they learn what to eat from their mother, who keeps a watchful eye on them at all times. With luck, they may have 30 years ahead of them.

The thawing taiga wetlands and waterways provide a welcome change of diet for the elks, which consume twice as much of the more palatable marsh grasses and water plants as they do of the bark and shoots which make up their winter diet. They stand up to their stomachs in the shallow marsh lakes, dipping their long snouts beneath the surface in search of succulent water plants and are joined in these wetter areas by a great variety of returning water birds such as the osprey (*Pandion haliaetus*) and whooper swan (*Cygnus cygnus*).

Since there is only a brief respite from the long snow and ice cover, the animals of the taiga concentrate on eating as much as possible in order to ensure their own energy levels and to produce viable young before the cold returns. If the winter has been especially harsh or spring late, many animals will have suffered and their populations will have declined. Plant growth will also be delayed and the year's harvest of fruits and seeds will be poor. However, if a mild winter is followed by an early spring, many animals will be much more numerous as a result of the lower winter mortality, and the year's fruits and seeds may well be abundant. In this way the taiga's animal populations fluctuate widely, especially when there are two or more consecutive very good or bad years.

Population fluctuations are particularly noticeable in those animals which reproduce rapidly and can take advantage of improved conditions, particularly rodents. Among the most common of these are the voles, such as the red vole (*Clethrionomys rutilus*) and the large-toothed red-backed vole (*C. rufocanus*), both found across Eurasia. Female voles can produce as many as five litters a year of up to eight young each: a maximum of 40 offspring from one vole, which, under good conditions, may each reproduce from the age of around two months. Thus the vole has an astounding reproductive potential and if conditions were absolutely ideal (for instance, in a warehouse full of grain) one pair could in theory produce after only two years a population of several hundred thousands or even millions – an astronomical population explosion. However, in the taiga, with predators and other adverse factors present, this staggering rate of population growth is impossible, and many of one year's new generation do not reproduce until the next and a good proportion of litters are small.

Just as in the case of the lemming of the tundra, tha taiga rodents' population fluctuations govern to a great extent the numbers of the predators which depend upon them. One such predator is the great grey owl (*Strix nebulosa*), one of the world's largest owls. It has a wingspan of about 5 ft (1.5 m) and a large, round head of about 20 in (50 cm) in diameter, almost the size of a human's, with plate-like discs around each yellow eye. Much of the bird's apparent bulk, however, is plumage and the body itself is

Bank voles feeding on berries, a fruit found in abundance and great variety throughout the taiga.

quite light. The owl feeds mostly on small mammals, and on occasion voles have been found to make up more than 90 percent of its diet. A glut of voles can greatly increase the owl's population by allowing more offspring and adults to survive to the next year. During periods of vole abundance clutches increase to nine eggs from the normal two to six.

The great grey owl usually occupies the old nests of other birds of prey, in some cases making minor repairs or adjustments. But this apparent lack of care is not evident in its defence of its young, and there are many instances of nasty injuries sustained by humans straying too close to a nest full of chicks, including people being knocked from trees and breaking their legs and others being blinded.

Like all owls the great grey has forward-facing eyes, which give it accurate vision and distance perception, but equally useful for this predator is its hearing. It has been observed to catch voles beneath 1 ft (30 cm) of snow, pinpointing them by its hearing alone. The bird perches or hovers near its intended prey and, when this has been accurately located, dives down and plunges its talons through the snow onto its unsuspecting victim.

In years of low vole numbers the owl is forced to search out different prey such as hares and hazel grouse. Food will be in particularly short supply if a good year with its multitude of voles is followed by a bad one, for then the owl's (and most other predators') populations will be high, putting great pressure on the dwindling prey. At times such as these many owls, especially younger birds in their first year, and other species perish as starvation takes its toll.

Autumn in the taiga is a time of preparation. Bears gorge themselves and search for suitable dens, nutcrackers and squirrels busy themselves amassing their winter provisions and vast flocks of birds depart for warmer climes. Once again the animals must suffer the long, dark nights and biting cold of a winter through which the old and unlucky will not survive.

Man himself does not feature at all in vast reaches of the taiga, other than the occasional hunter, trapper or fisherman along a remote river or geological team landed by helicopter. A map of the USSR's population density shows settlement in the taiga to be largely restricted to the south, with ribbons or pockets of habitation along the rivers and towns (some of them industrial) and villages scattered here and there, but with an almost empty – and gigantic – wilderness between.

Huge stretches of land may indeed be totally uninhabited but it is nonetheless the home of many different races and cultures which have lived here for centuries: Finno-Ugric peoples such as the Komi, distant relatives of the Lapps, west of the Urals; and east of that insignificant divide, the Khanty and Mansi, Samoyedic peoples such as the Selkup, Turkic peoples like the 327,000 Yakuts (also of the tundra) and the 600 Tofalary (both figures 1979), almost hidden in their dense southern mountain taiga, and Tungus-Manchus such as the Eveny and Evenky. All are traditionally fishing, hunting or herding peoples, and though they are now Russianized and intermarried (and in some cases 'endangered') to a greater or lesser extent, with varying proportions now in towns and some having their own intelligentsia, most remain ethnically and culturally distinct, their lifestyles adapted to the taiga on which they have been dependent for centuries.

There are Russians too: perhaps an isolated couple living in an *izba* or log house built with their own hands 30–40 years ago, living on the taiga's fish and game and nuts and berries, shooting squirrel and sable accurately through the eye to avoid damaging the pelt, the rivers their highway by boat in summer and sledge in winter.

Siberia's best-known novelist, Valentin Rasputin, has well described in his story 'Vasili and Vasilissa' one taiga-dweller's relationship with the great forest:

Vasili cannot live without the taiga. He knows it so well and loves it so much that one would think that he had created it himself, laid it out with his own hands and filled it with the treasures which it contains. In September he goes off gathering cedar pine nuts and knocks down cedar-cones right up until the snow comes. Then straightaway the hunting

Man-Pupy-Nyor, the northern Urals. These natural stone formations are found on the crest of the Ural mountains which rise above the taiga.

OPPOSITE *Splashes of colour are provided by the flora of the Urals. Fungi are found in profusion and many town dwellers make trips into the forest to gather edible mushrooms.*

season begins, Vasili goes off on two long hunting expeditions for squirrels and sables, once before the New Year and again after the New Year. In the Spring he looks for nuts again – when the snow has gone the cones which have fallen off the trees simply lie at your feet waiting to be picked up. In May you can pick bear's garlic, in July it is a sin not to fish for the red-and-black graylings of the taiga, in July the berries are ripe – and so on, year in, year out.

For such people the taiga provides the means of existence, food and shelter, but it also plays a large part in the lives of many city-dwellers. Fortunate to have a wilderness on their doorstep, for many urban Russians the forest is their countryside and part of their culture, and they love it passionately. In the European USSR 'the average annual recreational use of European forests is estimated . . . at approximately 11 billion hours per year; each inhabitant of this area spends an average of 71 hours per year enjoying the forest' (Brenton M. Barr and Kathleen E. Braden, *The Disappearing Russian Forest: A Dilemma in Soviet Resource Management*, Hutchinson, 1988).

Much of this time may well be spent gathering mushrooms, which the Russians love doing both as recreation and for their valuable nutrition, and forests provide 200 edible varieties. A few years ago a young Russian boy found one mushroom weighing 12 lb (5.5 kg), a feast for the hungriest of families. The forest also supplies, in good years, an abundance of berries and currants; indeed, more than 100 species of fruits, berries and nuts,

blackcurrant, redcurrant, cranberry and bilberry among them. Each year the state forestry enterprises (quite apart from the individual) produce 170,000 tons of fruit and berries (1986) which include the famous and highly nutritious nuts of the magnificent Siberian pine (*Pinus sibirica*) or 'cedar' as the Russians call it.

The taiga also supplies honey and birch juice, tapped from large birches and widely drunk, primarily as a health drink; more than 42,000 tons are produced annually. Birch juice is only one of the innumerable folk remedies that form a vital part of Soviet medicine, especially but by no means solely, in isolated areas. Closer to nature than Westerners – indeed in some cases living in its very midst – the peoples of the Soviet Union – not just of the taiga – have developed their own alternative medicine over centuries on which they often rely in the frequent absence of synthetic drugs and adequate health care. Indeed they may well prefer it, and plant medicines are sold in pharmacies as well as prepared at home.

As many as 2500 types of forest plant have been identified with curative properties for conditions from bronchitis to baldness, and 600 of them are used by the Soviet pharmaceutical industry. There exists a comprehensive 340-page atlas of the USSR's medicinal plants, published in 1976, itemizing in great detail all botanical, chemical and medicinal properties. One example is sallowthorn or sea buckthorn (*Hippophae sibirica*), a shrub 7–10 ft (2–3 m) high which is a rich source of vitamins, especially C and E, with smaller amounts of B1 and B2. An oil from its seeds and berries is used by modern therapy to rejuvenate tissue, treat burns, wounds, frostbite, eczema and inflammation. Another example is 'golden root' (*Rhodiola rosea*), a grass-like plant with thick golden roots, known for centuries to Siberian shamans and used both in the USSR and North America, where it also grows, as a tonic or stimulant and to treat headaches, insomnia and nervous illness. Centuries of experience should surely not be ignored by Western medicine and at the very least deserve examination. Who knows what the taiga could produce for the benefit of mankind?

The taiga is also a valuable source of meat, and the forest-dwellers hunt for their own needs, the state's or the local market. But over the past century such hunting has dwindled to second place after hunting for sport. In moderation, the latter does not harm the ecosystem or reduce animal numbers. But the situation is now out of control, and more than one in ten adult males in the whole country – around eight million people – hunt for sport, with obvious consequences. Earlier this century an estimated five to six million hazel grouse alone were caught annually and as a result their numbers started to decline.

But the grouse is only one of man's many sporting prey, alongside ducks, geese, bears, wild boars and elks. Restrictions are frequently ignored even by officials, and poaching can perhaps be regarded as one of the few areas of the Soviet economy to have enjoyed steady growth of late. Such activities are inevitable in a country where meat is difficult and expensive to obtain, but some hunting is totally indiscriminate and inexcusable. For years there have been stories of government ministers, party officials and high-ranking officers hunting in protected nature reserves, a practice one hopes has now ended.

The striking symmetry of a silver birch forest in the Ural mountains. Birch juice is widely tapped and consumed as a health drink.

But it is a question of attitude also. In his eye-opening book *The Destruction of Nature in the Soviet Union* (Pluto Press, 1978) Boris Komarov (the pseudonym of Zeev Wolfson) wrote that 'our rocket officers [stationed near Lake Baikal] reasoned quite soberly that they could find no better targets for training troops to shoot ground-to-ground heat-seeking missiles at than wild boar and deer on the run. Startled by the sound of a shot, the animals dash across the wooded hills, and the accurate rockets overtake them wherever they go.'

Komarov also records that:

In 1898 the exiled populist Iokhelson published a book in Petersburg in which he . . . distinguished three kinds of hunters in the Siberian North. The first was the traditional local hunter, essentially a pagan; the second was the old Russian peasant entrepreneur who tries to profit from hunting but never kills animals senselessly and leaves breeding stock. The third kind is new folk without religious principles, who come for the season and kill everything in sight, even more than they can carry away and sell. They shoot animals not for money but for amusement, for sheer pleasure . . .

This third, rapacious type has spread like the plague in the twentieth century. Neither the old Christian morality nor the new communist ideals make any impression on him.

Komarov goes on to quote from a Russian writer, Vladimir Sapozhnikov, describing in the 1970s the current situation: 'Just give hunters trained in [shooting] galleries a chance, and they will turn everything that crawls, flies, breathes, and sings into a meal . . .'

Given this outlook, it is hardly surprising that poaching continues, particularly since one sable pelt, for instance, can be worth as much as US$1000 and a skilful, hard-working trapper can earn five times the average Soviet wage in one winter. The Soviet Union's bitter winters, incidentally,

legitimize the wearing of utilitarian fur coats and the anti-fur lobby is unlikely to gain much ground here. Luxury furs, including the sable, are almost all destined for North America and Europe, where increasingly they are ethically unacceptable.

It may therefore be that without a commercial demand the sable, of which some quarter of a million are caught each year, may along with Russia's other fur bearers revert to its original numbers of centuries ago – or could there even be a population explosion? Perhaps too, the fur farms, which produce so much less laboriously many thousands of pelts a year from small individual cages, will also ultimately be phased out.

On an infinitely smaller commercial scale and operated more on an experimental basis are the elk farms, which aim to provide small quantities of dairy products and meat. Elk milk is claimed to be five times as rich in protein as cow's milk, and butter can be made from it without the need to separate the cream. The animals are left to graze in the taiga and, easily tamed, they can pull heavily laden sledges in winter and supply meat particularly rich in protein. The elk farmers have to take care not to overstock the forest with elk, however, for if too many are kept in one place they can eat all the seedlings and a great deal of bark, thus killing some trees and allowing no others to grow in their place. For this reason a maximum of one elk per 400 acres (160 ha) has been suggested, which means a massive area for a sizeable herd – as well as quite a problem at milking time. So elk farming is unlikely ever to be a major operation.

While hunting and trapping (and elk farming) all exert varying degrees of pressure on the taiga's ecology, their effect is nothing like those of forest fires and man's deforestation and degradation. Natural fires, started by lightning strikes, certainly help to maintain the diversity of the taiga, for trees such as the birch colonize the newly opened areas and after some years the shade-tolerant conifers grow up beneath the birch canopy, eventually overtopping them to dominate the tree composition once again. But fires have now greatly increased, and the culprit is nearly always man. In 1989 an astounding 28,000 forest fires were recorded across the country, almost all of them in the taiga, enveloping a total of 6180 square miles (16,000 sq km).

Askold Yakubovsky writes of one fire caused by man in his story 'A meeting in the forest':

> The sight of stretches of burned down forest is truly blood-chilling. The flames have devoured everything, the needles first, then the branches and finally the trunks. And charred remains stand like black spectres.
>
> Everything is dead. There is no stirring of life, no voices, only the wind now playing a mournful melody on the black keyboard of the charred trunks, now striking a blackened tree in a fit of temper, making it heave a tired sigh, bend over, and lie down with a crunching sound.

The taiga has not evolved to cope with the frequency of such fires and in many areas the conifer-dominated forest does not have enough time between fires to re-establish itself, with far-reaching repercussions for the conifer-dependent wildlife. Although the Soviet Union has a sophisticated force of forest-fire-fighters, sometimes dropped in by parachute, the ultimate answer is to educate the citizens in greater responsibility.

Young elks at an elk farm, eager to be fed. Elk milk is said to be five times richer in protein than that of cows, but the farming is on a limited scale at present.

Over the centuries people have been eroding the taiga for settlement and cultivation. Today the state is by far the greatest 'predator' of the nation's forests, above all the taiga, extracting each year almost half a billion cubic yards (0.38 billion cu m.) of unprocessed wood – the equivalent of a 'log' 30 ft (9 m) in diameter stretching from London to New York. The Soviet Union is now the world's biggest timber-producing nation, but unfortunately the vastness of the taiga and an understandable belief in its inexhaustibility have all too often meant clear felling and, until recently, often little or no reafforestation. Soil erosion has resulted from felling on slopes, rivers have become silted up and filled with millions of sunken logs which poison the water, kill the fish, thus reducing the birds that feed on them, and endanger navigation. Much of the taiga may remain untouched, but 304 million acres (138 million ha) – two and a half times the size of France – has already been severely degraded.

Regeneration is particularly slow in the harsh environment of eastern Siberia, for once the soil is laid bare permafrost frequently creeps up to the surface and no saplings can take root or grow. The long swath cut through just this taiga by the construction in the 1970s and 1980s of the Baikal–Amur Mainline (BAM) railway and the consequent development of the area have brought major problems of degradation across an enormous belt, while other economic activities have also laid waste sizeable tracts of land.

In some areas air pollution is killing the taiga. According to official Soviet figures, 310 square miles (810 sq km) of taiga has been affected round the industrial town of Bratsk, 2100 square miles (5450 sq km) round Norilsk, and at Satka in the Urals 40 square miles (104 sq km) of forest has completely died round one industrial complex within a damaged (but now fortunately stabilized) total area of 190 sq miles (500 sq km).

Once more, therefore, we must be grateful to the system of nature reserves which protect or restore the taiga's pristine nature. Many of them are beautiful sites, such as Lake Baikal's Barguzin reserve, founded in 1916, before the Revolution. In places in this reserve the ancient silver and spruce firs are 100 ft (30 m) tall, forming a fine stretch of taiga sweeping down from the mountains to the edge of the lake: home to bears, sables and the elegant flying squirrel with its nests high in the trees above.

Such reserves, together with increasing concern for the environment and the effects of perestroika, bring some hope for Russia's magnificent taiga heritage and its wildlife, although its timber remains an obvious source of the hard currency so badly needed at present and there remains a strong temptation to over-exploit it. Perhaps the present changes will bring a more efficient lumber industry operating on a sustainable forestry system.

In conclusion, how odd it is to reflect that the gigantic belt of forest that is the taiga lies south of the tundra's totally treeless (other than dwarf species) ecosystem and north of another ecosystem almost totally treeless and far better known to the rest of the world than the forests. This latter expanse, the steppe, has its own, totally different, wildlife, its own land use, history, peoples, cultures, patterns of settlement and environmental problems.

Thomas Schultze-Westrum, cameraman in the Pechoro-Ilych Nature Reserve, west of the Northern Urals

One day we walked through very variable forest, often becoming soaked from falling into large water holes covered in moss. Clearings had been created by natural fires and then covered once again by beautiful birch forests.

There are exquisite colours in the forest, bright green moss contrasting with the various oranges and reds. The leaves there are beautiful and change within a few days. The ash trees move in the wind, producing a very exciting noise. Leaves fall to the ground – more and more of them – making a wonderful pattern of yellow against the green moss and the pale mushrooms. There are mushrooms everywhere, but they are too expensive to transport. People collect them, mostly for their own consumption, frying them over fires.

Traditional methods are still used in places for the construction of houses which are built from local carved wood. The logs, with notched ends, are tied together in a circular shape. The base is made from moss and the roof constructed from boards and shingle.

The *yatkon* cattle are ridden and are also used for dragging heavy loads through the snow; in the summer they are used mainly for milking. The local people believe that the cattle are very 'emotional' animals; little children talk constantly to the cows which would apparently answer in soft, melodic tones.

I visited an elk station; these stations are the only places in the Soviet Union where these animals are domesticated. They are used for milking, pulling sledges and for dragging timber in the snow. They are also ridden. Baby elk are so affectionate towards their keepers, always following them whilst making 'Mmm' noises.

CHAPTER FOUR

THE TREELESS STEPPE

The farther they went, the more beautiful became the steppe . . . At that time all the south . . . was a green virgin wilderness. Never had plough passed over the immeasurable waves of wild growth; only the horses, hidden in it as in a wood, trampled it down. Nothing in Nature could be finer. The whole surface of the earth was a green-gold ocean splashed with millions of different coloured flowers.

Much has changed since Gogol wrote his story 'Taras Bulba' over 150 years ago. Almost all the steppe has come under the plough; many of the wild flowers have become extinct; human population is dense, particularly in the west; and the tractor is now far more common than the horse. But the essential and seemingly endless flat and treeless plain remains an important factor in Russian history and psychology.

The famous steppe, an enormous expanse of grassland before its cultivation, forms a vast belt 200–600 miles (320–970 km) wide, stretching uninterruptedly all the way from Hungary and the lower Danube, through the Ukraine and the south of European Russia and on eastwards across the huge republic of Kazakhstan to the Altai foothills of southern Siberia. There are even isolated patches beyond, along the borders with Mongolia and China.

There is no forest here, because the light rainfall – only short but heavy showers, producing a sea of mud – prevents its growth. The great steppe therefore, along with the climatically similar North American prairies, South American pampas, South African veldt and tropical savannah,

Graceful feathergrasses thrive on the southern steppes.

A long-legged juvenile demoiselle crane.

constitutes the earth's natural grasslands, comprising just over a quarter (27 percent) of its natural vegetation cover – at least it did before man's disturbance.

Geologically speaking, this is some of the most ancient land in the USSR, dating back to the Pliocene era seven to ten million years ago. In the southern steppe, increasing aridity produces ever poorer – chestnut and brown soils – until steppe eventually gives way to the semi-desert and desert of Kazakhstan and the Central Asian republics. But the great mass of the steppe is chernozem, the black earth used internationally as a result of the pioneering work of nineteenth-century Russian soil scientists.

This is some of the richest soil in the world, so rich that it can produce crops for many years without the use of fertilizers and obviously unrivalled for cereal production. P. S. Pallas, the famous eighteenth-century German naturalist and a pioneer of Russian natural history, made a long expedition through southern Russia (and Siberia). He wrote that 'in this district of rich black soil . . . the happy husbandman has no occasion to manure his grounds, and commonly fallows his land but every third crop . . . Was this rich ground to be manured, the corn would be luxuriant and full.'

Chernozem covers around one tenth of the land area of the Soviet Union and is the largest continuous expanse of black earth on the planet. It has been called 'one of the world's most valuable natural resources, worth more than coal or oil or gold', and the German occupying forces in the Second World War are said to have carried off Ukrainian topsoil by the trainload.

Black earth is in some places over 3 ft (1 m) deep and owes its richness to a high content of humus above a deep layer of lime-rich and easily worked silts which developed during the last glaciation at the edge of the ice sheet and was blown south by winds on to the ice-free steppe. The humus itself is due to the alliance of climate and the steppe's natural vegetation: a lush cover of grasses and flowering herbs, particularly dense in the north's meadow steppe. The slow decay of this dense network of grass produces rich organic matter, which is then dug over by an army of burrowing rodents and fertilized by their droppings. As a result, there is intense bacterial activity each spring, releasing nitrogen, calcium and other plant nutrients which remain close to the surface.

The continental climate, with its hot, dry summers and cold winters, means that frosts slow down the decomposition of plant material during the winter, while water is retained so that grasses grow abundantly in spring. The dryness responsible for the treeless nature of the steppe helps the soil to retain its goodness by preventing leaching.

Plants which live on the steppe have to be able to survive extremes of climate. They must be both frost- and drought-resistant and have adapted in many different ways to the demands of their environment. Some species, such as the graceful feather grasses (*Stipa*) which dominate the southern steppes, have developed a kind of hairy, felt-like down which traps a layer of air and so reduces water loss through evaporation. Other plants have waxy leaves which act to retain moisture and prevent excessive evaporation or vestigial leaves with a small surface area and deep roots. Apart from the feather grasses, typical plants of the steppe include various types of fescues (*Festuca*), sedges, two types of wormwood or sagebrush (*Artemisia graciliscens* and *A. sublessingia*) and wild onion (*Allium rotundum*). There are also numerous wild flowers (others have become extinct) that transform the virgin steppe in spring and summer, and one observer in spring has described how it changes colour with the changing plant life: purple with plumbago at the end of March, yellow with primulas and primroses in April and blue with forget-me-nots in May.

From time immemorial, nomadic tribes have wandered the steppe, seeking pasture for their flocks and waging war on one another. Goths and Varangians came from the west, Huns, Avars, Khazars, Scythians and Mongols, among others, from the east, with the result that cultivation of the steppe was hindered by constant incursions and upheavals. The steppe peoples, notably the Scythians and much later the Cossacks, became renowned for their horsemanship, developed so ideally on these flat plains. The Scythians also left behind them scattered landmarks, stone statues of a woman, probably depicting the great goddess of fertility, which still stand on the steppe today.

Russia conquered its way free of the 'Tatar yoke' in the sixteenth century, gaining the south-eastern steppe and then, a century later, by treaty, the steppe of the eastern Ukraine, and in the eighteenth century the final amount by annexation. Often the Cossack settlements acted as the expanding Russian Empire's frontier troops on the 'New Russia' of the open steppe, but Catherine the Great, wanting to secure her frontiers against the wandering Kalmyks, Kirgiz and others and colonize the empty grasslands, invited settlers, in particular hard-working Germans, Dutch and French, to cultivate the steppe around the lower Volga in 1763, offering free land and no taxation or conscription.

The first settlers, with notable exceptions, did little better than the Russian peasants among whom they lived, but later German settlers who cultivated areas near the Black Sea became very prosperous. By the 1840s there were military colonies, too, of some 60,000 men on the southern steppe, supplying the Russian cavalry both with men and horses; and hussars and cuirassiers in full uniform could be seen, according to J. G. Kohl's *Russia*, published in 1842, 'with their sabres at their sides, labouring behind the plough or driving their wild herds over the grassy steppes'.

Travelling across the 'verdant ocean', Kohl found Bulgarian colonists the most industrious, far more so than the Germans, some of them owning 7–12,000 oxen and huge flocks of sheep. But the early days of settlement were no sinecure and there was always the threat of drought. It took one party of German colonists a year and a half to reach the steppe, and many died from infectious illnesses *en route*. On arrival, they found uninhabitable houses – better at least than the dug-outs which the first pioneers had to construct – and useless agricultural implements; nor had they any idea of when to plough or when or what to sow. Furthermore, knowing no Russian, they could learn nothing from the Russian settlers. Kohl nonetheless estimated there were nearly a quarter of a million German colonists on the steppe in the 1840s and found some wealthy colonies where the richest members owned up to 20,000 sheep: 'all Merinos, or of some other fine breed and the orchards promised such an abundant crop, that the trees had to be propped up under the weight of their rich burden.'

The abolition of serfdom in 1861 brought a wave of new settlers to the steppe when freed serfs, understanding very little about agriculture, began to farm in communal strips, ignoring the contours of the land. The result was the first appearance of soil erosion, a problem which has grown to worrying proportions today.

However, the steppe's first problem is lack of water and its second problem early frosts, so it is ironic that famine has stalked across the world's most fertile soils. According to one early chronicler:

> In the year 1230, on 14 September, the frost killed the grain in our lands, which caused much distress . . . People left the town and region . . . those who remained began to starve. Who would not shed tears, seeing dead bodies lying in the streets, and infants eaten by dogs? So God put it into the heart of Archbishop Spiridon to . . . [have] a burial pit dug out . . . and [he] appointed a good and humble man, Stanilo by name, to bring the dead on a horse as he went round the town. Stanilo brought them constantly every day, and the pit was filled to the top: three thousand and thirty persons were buried in it.

In the late nineteenth century increasingly frequent drought brought a succession of crop failures resulting, in 1891–2, in the worst famine for a century, in which nearly half a million people died. Crop failures in 1901 led

The Kalmyk steppe today, now threatened by desertification.

to serious disturbances and in the two succeeding years, thousands of hungry peasants in three southern provinces plundered the barns of the gentry.

Famine returned on a terrible scale in 1921. Then in 1929 Stalin began the forced collectivization of agriculture which was to merge 25 million peasant holdings across the country into about 200,000 enormous collective farms or *kolkhozy* and state farms (*sovkhozy*). The peasants rebelled, and slaughtered and ate their livestock, fearing it would be confiscated, and millions of them – including the so-called kulaks or better-off peasants (who, we might surmise, were the better farmers) – were dispossessed and sent to distant labour camps.

The whole process of collectivization claimed at least 6 million peasants' lives throughout the country, with up to another 7.5 million dying from the consequent famine, which was partially, it has been claimed, engineered by the state to break their resistance. Grain was ruthlessly requisitioned down to the smallest hidden morsel, food was confiscated at the Ukraine's borders, which were sealed to prevent the starving populace leaving, and at the same time grain exports were enormously increased in order to obtain the foreign currency essential for industrialization. By 1937, 93 percent of the (remaining) peasants had been collectivized – an enormous agricultural revolution at immense human cost.

Collectivization brought to the steppe the large-scale mechanization of agriculture, so that harvesting was done much more thoroughly and fields left much barer, both practices depriving wildlife of its habitat and leaving the land more vulnerable to erosion. Despite new technology and an increase in the sown area, collectivization imposed a basically unworkable and inefficient system ruled by Moscow's politicians and bureaucrats rather than by local farmers.

Furthermore, the disastrously incompetent distribution system meant – and, alas, still means – that even after a bumper harvest a huge proportion of grain is likely to rot somewhere along the line. We must not discount the steppe's problems of drought and early frost, but nonetheless the result is that for many years the Soviet Union has had to import massive quantities of American, Canadian and Australian grain. Indeed this year (1991) US President George Bush has approved the $1.5 billion (£903 million) agricultural credit guarantees which President Gorbachev had urgently requested.

It was not until 1954, when Khrushchev began his Virgin and Long Idle Lands Project, however, that most of the remaining virgin steppe was lost. Khrushchev wanted to grow enough grain to feed the population, and in two years nearly 90 million acres (35 million ha) of land came under the plough. Although he acknowledged the climate's erratic nature, even allowing for only two good harvests out of every five because of drought, wind erosion became acute and soils which had taken hundreds of years to build up were sometimes, without their cover of vegetation, devastated in a few minutes by winds, especially those of a strong and desiccating kind, which developed into dust storms.

It is estimated that when such ground is bare, even light winds of 20–30 ft (6–9 m) per second can lift off 9 tons of topsoil from 2½ acres (1 ha) of land in half an hour. In 1964, on the Khakassian steppe, at the eastern end of the main band of the steppe lands, the situation became so desperate that ploughing was forbidden altogether.

Since then, to rectify matters, windbreaks of trees have been planted (although the necessary irrigation for the trees brings salts to the surface, causing another problem), fields have been ploughed at right angles to the wind and, following the practice of American prairie farmers, stubble has been left on the ground to anchor the soil. Mixed farming practices have been introduced. Even so, at present as much as two thirds of agricultural land in the Soviet Union is in areas affected by wind or other erosion.

The cultivated steppe now sustains dairy cattle, pigs, poultry and sheep and, besides cereal crops, produces sunflowers, melons, cucumbers and, in damper areas at the edge of the wooded steppe, sugar beet. Wheat, however, is the major crop (with maize in second place) and the Ukraine, almost all steppe and wooded steppe, has long been known as 'the granary' of the Soviet Union – the ultimate accolade in a land whose traditional greeting and symbol of life are based on bread and salt.

However, vestiges at least of the original steppe remain, even if largely confined now to nature reserves. The oldest of these, indeed the oldest in the country, is Askaniya-Nova in the southern Ukrainian steppe. It was originally established in 1878 by Friedrich Falz-Fein, an extremely wealthy and innovative landowner, descendant of a German who had fled to Russia in 1763 and taken up Catherine the Great's invitation to foreign settlers to colonize the steppe.

Askaniya-Nova was originally conceived as a sheep farm (using dried sheep dung to make sheep enclosures on the empty steppe), but Falz-Fein envisioned an 'animal paradise'. He started in 1884 with one flock of birds, one bear, one wolf, one roe deer and one white hare in a single enclosure but began to import animals and birds from comparable habitats throughout the world. By 1914 he had 58 species of mammals and 402 types of birds, with herds of zebra, bison, lamas, gnus, antelopes, gazelles, camels, ostriches and other exotic animals grazing on the steppe, watched over by mounted shepherds. The estate had its own sophisticated irrigation system with a water tower and pumps bringing 300,000 bucketfuls of water a day from the River Dnieper; on them everything depended.

Inevitably, success came only after major problems. Once there was a terrible dust storm from the parched steppe; once a plague of locusts. On another occasion a sudden cold spell immediately after shearing froze 30,000 sheep to death.

Between 1898 and 1903 Falz-Fein succeeded in bringing to his zoo park 11 Przewalski's horses (*Equus przewalskii*), the first to be brought to Europe from Asia. This was a great coup, for the horse had long been thought extinct, being known only from Palaeolithic cave paintings in France and Spain. Then, in the late nineteenth century, the Russian explorer Przewalski, who had heard rumours of its existence, discovered a herd in Mongolia. It is significant as the earliest species of horse still extant and the only living ancestor of today's domestic horse: smaller, stocky, dun-coloured with a dark stripe down the back, an erect mane and long tail. Alas, Askaniya-Nova's Przewalskis were all destroyed in the Second World

Tarpans were once abundant on the steppe but now, sadly, are extinct. However, the species has been 'reconstituted' from domesticated breeds of horses and can now be found in areas of northern Europe.

War, although examples in other zoos have survived and there are now plans to return the animal to its native home in Mongolia in 1993 to be released in the wild.

Falz-Fein was particularly interested in cross-breeding and began to produce new hybrids of cows, sheep and pigs. In 1910 he pioneered the first centre to work on the artificial insemination of horses. It was to become in 1932 the Institute of Hybridization and produced the first cross ever between a horse and zebra.

The achievements at Askaniya-Nova were widely recognized and indeed two Tsars paid the estate a visit: Alexander II and later, in 1914, Nicholas II, who elevated the family to the hereditary nobility. But only months after Nicholas's visit, the First World War began and Germans in Russia – even those of distant German origin – were penalized and all German property confiscated. Then, following the Revolution in 1917, Falz-Fein was arrested as an aristocrat, but released after representations from, among others, the head of Moscow Zoo and fled back to Germany, where he died in 1920.

During the civil war of 1918–20 Askaniya-Nova found itself caught between Reds and Whites, both of whom killed the animals for food. By the time the Bolshevik commander (later the 'legendary' Marshal) Budyonny had captured the area and the fighting had stopped, almost three quarters of the animals had been lost. Under the new Soviet power, it became a state nature reserve.

During the Second World War, the site was once again overrun. The land was dug up and spoilt by military activity and most of the animals were requisitioned as food. When the German occupation ended in 1943, all the scientific records had been lost or destroyed and only 20 percent of the animals remained. Once more Askaniya-Nova had to be recreated but by the end of the 1950s it had become a fully-fledged scientific research institute with a large staff and an improvement grant of 5 million roubles.

Askaniya-Nova was given nature-reserve status in 1921 and designated a Biosphere Reserve in 1984. Today it embraces 43 square miles (111 sq km) and contains the last 6 square miles (15 sq km) of Europe's virgin feather-grass steppe.

What distinguishes Askaniya-Nova from all other present-day zoological gardens is its exceptional collection of 60 different ungulates or hoofed mammals. The world's first and only antelope farm is here and boasts the only milking elands (South African antelope) to be found anywhere. The milk, which contains three times the amount of fat and twice the protein of cow's milk, is now sold commercially. A new medicine has been developed from it and is used to speed the healing of wounds and to treat tuberculosis and gastric ulcers.

First opened to the public in 1912, Askaniya-Nova welcomed 13,000 visitors by 1917. Now 200,000 arrive every year, attracted not only by the animals but also by another unique feature, the 'dendropark', a remarkable botanical garden in the middle of the steppe with more than 1000 species of trees and bushes, nearly 2000 species of grasses and 450 steppe plants, 56 of them endangered.

The reserve's size also protects 57 species of mammal and 213 of birds. It is the only place in the Ukraine where the steppe eagle (*Aquila rapax*) still nests. The bird's population may be nationwide in the tens of thousands, but its numbers are rapidly declining and it is included in Appendix II of CITES (Convention on International Trade in Endangered Species of Wild Fauna and Flora). The eagle arrives in spring from its wintering grounds in Africa, the Middle East, India and China and starts constructing or renovating its eyrie, some 3 ft (1 m) in diameter and built perforce on the ground or, in recent years, also on straw stacks, electricity pylons and telegraph poles, before laying a clutch of usually two eggs in late April which hatch in June.

Adult steppe eagles feed mainly on medium-sized rodents such as susliks, but they are also fond of big-eared hedgehogs, snakes, carrion and other birds' fledglings. They hunt the suslik by stalking along the ground or by standing still at the entrance to its burrow and ambushing the unwitting rodent as it comes out to feed.

Juvenile steppe eagles. The eggs of this rare predator hatch at the beginning of June in nests built upon the ground as there are no trees. These eaglets are sometimes fed young, weak saiga antelope and the skull of one can be seen in the foreground.

Like the steppe eagle, the two bustards of the steppe have the unfortunate distinction of being included as endangered species in the USSR's own Red Data Book. The great bustard (*Otis tarda tarda*) is one of the largest birds in the world. The male, larger than the female, has been known to weigh up to an extraordinary 46 lb (21 kg), although it averages around 20–22 lb (9–10 kg), and has characteristic filiform feathers on each side of its head which give the distinct impression of whiskers. The species has two population ranges, one in the western steppe of around 2300 birds and one in the eastern Siberian steppe of 500–600. Its numbers have dropped dramatically in recent decades, for instance from 2000 birds in the Saratov region in 1978 to only 683 nests two years later.

Poaching, pesticides and the intensification of agriculture are among the culprits as they are also in the case of the little bustard (*Otis tetrax*), which has totally disappeared from Moldavia (now Moldova) in the west. Its overall population, however, is relatively stable and indeed up from between 4800 and 8000 in 1978–80 to 13,000–16,800 in the mid 1980s. Unrestricted hunting has nonetheless driven it from many areas.

Both bustards are quiet and very timid and are therefore fortunate in having speed. At the first sight of danger they shoot vertically into the air, and they can fly fast: at about 40 mph (65 kmph) when low over the ground and at an average 47–50 mph (75–80 kmph) on long flights. On the ground they can run as fast as a man. They also make full use of their protective colouring and are very adept at concealing themselves and blending into

Although one of the largest birds in the world, the great bustard is very timid and shoots vertically into the air if threatened. The male makes full use of its colouring and decorative plumes and bristles in mating displays.

their surroundings – just as well, considering their size. The female sensibly excavates a shallow hollow in which to lay her eggs in order to be hardly above ground level and thus as inconspicuous as possible.

In contrast to the bustards, the plover (*Chettusia gregaria*) makes no effort to conceal its existence. The latter part of its name accurately depicts a lively, noisy bird which likes living in groups. Endemic to the USSR, it used to be common across large areas of the Ukraine and Kazakhstan, but it is now very rare as a result of the cultivation of the steppe.

Perhaps the most beautiful bird of the steppe is the graceful demoiselle crane (*Anthropoides virgo*), which is smaller than other cranes and is characterized by its conspicuous white ear tufts, black neck and breast and lack of red on the head. Like all cranes, it flies in V-formation, but with one leg of the V much longer than the other. When migrating to winter in Africa and India (it returns to the Ukraine in late March or early April) it flies so high as to be almost invisible, although its call can still be heard.

In common with all other cranes it forms permanent monogamous pairs, and immediately on arrival at the nesting site, the same year after year, it begins its courtship displays, which have been termed 'crane balls' because of the elegance of the dances and their communal performance. Positioning themselves in a circle, sometimes up to three rows deep, the cranes watch while a few birds in the centre of the circle begin to dance, leaping upwards with wings and necks outstretched. The dancers then extend their long necks, bowing this way and that, spreading out their crop feathers and

The demoiselle crane, one of the smallest of the species, has distinctive white plumes on the back of its head and extremely graceful, agile neck movements.

making trumpeting calls. When tired, they return to the audience and are replaced by cranes which have not yet danced.

The pairs disperse and the female crane usually lays two eggs in a makeshift nest on the ground about 2–2½ miles (3–4 km) from the nearest neighbour. Only in August do the scattered family units become flocks once more as they prepare to fly south. Poaching and pesticides plus the tilling and degradation of the steppe are affecting its numbers (45–50,000 at last count) and 200–700 nestlings are exported to zoos annually even though the bird is in the USSR's Red Data Book.

Among the steppe's endemic birds are the black and white-winged larks (*Melanocorypha yeltoniensis* and *M. leucoptera*), the second of which has strayed as far as the British Isles. The larger black lark is unusually beautiful in flight, flapping its wings almost vertically.

The rarest bird of the steppe and wooded steppe is unquestionably the endemic slenderbilled curlew (*Numenius tenuirostris*), with no records of breeding birds being seen in the Soviet Union for over 60 years. Judging from the numbers observed wintering in Morocco over the years, it is in steep decline: 800 birds in 1964, 123 individuals in 1975, and now only two or three a year. No one knows where they come from, but ornithologists regard them as on the edge of extinction, with between 100 and 1000 left.

In happier contrast, there are at least healthy populations of other steppe birds, including quails, pipits, finches and pratincoles. While these live on the surface of the steppe, a very different population makes its home beneath: a veritable army of rodents, particularly ground squirrels known as susliks. The most common of the five species is the little suslik (*Citellus pygmaeus*), also known as 'the whistler' because of the characteristic danger signal which it usually emits while standing bolt upright and looking keenly about it with its front paws pressed to its chest.

The little suslik appears to have remained unperturbed by the cultivation of the virgin steppe and indeed thrives on the cereal crops, particularly wheat, corn and millet, which man considerately grows on its territory. Unfortunately, man therefore regards this rodent as a pest and tries to get rid of it in the cultivated steppe, not surprisingly, since one little suslik is estimated to consume 9 lb (4 kg) of cereals each year. A well-known Soviet biologist S. I. Ognev, wrote in 1963 that the total area inhabited by the little suslik is 154,000 square miles (400,000 sq km) and the average density is 37 animals per acre (15 per ha). This, he calculated, gives the astronomical total of 600 million little susliks devouring 2.4 million tons (2.44 million tonnes) of grain per year.

Like all sensible rodents on the steppe, the little suslik hibernates during the long, cold winter, to emerge drowsily with the onset of spring. A few days later the mating season begins and may continue for up to 25 days. Squeaking loudly, the males chase the females, which dive for cover into the nearest burrow. After a month's pregnancy the female gives birth to an average of six young, who come into the world naked and blind and take about two weeks to develop fur and emerge from the burrow. They then spend their days playing and basking in the warm sun, and towards the end of summer fatten themselves up along with their elders in order to sleep through the winter.

Unlike the suslik, the sandy-coloured bobac marmot (*Marmota bobac*), does not damage man's crops, but restricts its diet to wild plants, including steppe grasses and wild onions, and gains its necessary intake of moisture from its food and the morning dew. Numbering about 1.25 million, considerably less than the little suslik, this is the only marmot to inhabit steppe rather than mountain.

Until the eighteenth century the bobac was very common, but the ploughing of the virgin steppe drove it from its traditional habitat, and extensive hunting for its fur and excellent meat also had a severe effect on its numbers. So too did the famines of the late nineteenth century as well as the civil war and the Second World War, when it was eaten by the starving population. However, since the banning of bobac hunting in most areas, its numbers have increased and it has adapted itself abandoned settlements, usually deserted by people for the town.

With its short, strong legs and stumpy tail, the bobac may look rather fat and clumsy, but it is capable of moving very fast. Its burrows are extremely complex, often with six or seven entrances and sometimes 10–16 feet (3–5 m) deep. Some burrows are for living in, some for escaping to quickly and some, near the entrance, serve as latrines.

As a creature of habit, the bobac prefers to stay in the same place year after year and its presence is clearly indicated both by 'bobac mounds', piles of recently excavated earth which dot its terrain, and patches of dark-green vegetation noticeable in the summer's dried steppe. At the end of August and the beginning of September the bobacs congregate in their sleeping chambers for hibernation, during which they can lose up to 35 percent of their body weight. But first they plug the entrances to their burrows with a

Przewalski's horse, seen here in Poland, but currently being reintroduced into Russia after near-extinction. The reintroduction programme should be well under way by 1993.

mixture of earth, excrement and stones which helps to ensure that the temperature inside never falls below freezing even during the worst frosts.

Like most other steppe inhabitants, the bobac's primary sense is its eyesight. Even fog makes it feel insecure and forces it back into its burrow, whereas the common hamster (*Cricetus cricetus*), another typical steppe inhabitant, is nocturnal, relying heavily on its acute hearing and sense of smell and appearing very seldom during the day. Over 1 ft (30 cm) long, with black belly, sandy-brown back and white paws, it is both larger and more colourful than the golden hamster kept as a domestic pet.

Unlike the bobac and the little suslik, it is a solitary animal which can be extremely aggressive towards members of its own species – not unlike *Homo sapiens* in that respect. Its numbers have declined as a result of the ploughing up of the virgin steppe, even though the female common hamster is sexually mature at 43 days (compared to three years for the bobac marmot) and can give birth after only 59 days, producing two to three litters of up to ten or more young from April to October.

Like other hamsters, the common hamster has cheek pouches in which it carries food back to its burrow, and with the onset of autumn it fills its storage chambers with up to 44 lb (20 kg) of vegetation on which to feed when it wakes occasionally from its hibernation. These pouches also prove invaluable when crossing rivers, when it inflates them as built-in water wings.

Most of the numerous other rodents living on the steppe, including species of lemming, mouse and vole, are common animals as they adapt fairly well to new habitats and their reproduction rate soon replenishes the population. It is instead the larger animals which are often most at risk, and one species has already been lost. Until the mid nineteenth century the steppe saw whole herds of tarpan (known to some zoologists as *Equus ferus*), a mouse-grey wild horse with thick head, pointed ears and short, frizzy mane, but, as the steppe was ploughed up and man's livestock competed for the dwindling grasslands, the tarpan became doomed and the last one died on an estate in the Ukraine in 1918.

We might wonder why the tarpan was not saved from extinction by Askaniya-Nova. One ungulate which was protected there and could well have perished otherwise is the saiga antelope (*Saiga tatarica*), which fossil remains show to have been a contemporary of the woolly mammoth and to have grazed all the way between Britain and Alaska. Although commonly referred to as an antelope, the saiga has evolved independently over several million years and looks more like a sheep or goat. Only about 3 ft (1 m) high (2 ft 5 in/73 cm at the withers) – the female is slightly smaller – and 100 lb (45 kg) in weight, the male has 1 ft (30 cm) long ringed/twisted horns, slightly lyre-shaped and pale pinkish-amber in colour.

The saiga's most distinctive feature is its unique nose, which is extremely large, soft and trumpet-shaped, and droops down so far over the muzzle that the saiga has to wrinkle it up to one side when eating. Extraordinary it may be in appearance, but the saiga's nose is a classic example of environmental adaptation. In summer, when the great saiga herds cross the baked landscape at speeds of anything up to 50 mph (72 kmph), raising enormous clouds of dust with their heads only 3 ft (1 m) or so off the ground, the nose acts as an extremely efficient filter, keeping dust and sand

from the animal's lungs, while in winter it warms and moistens the freezing air. The secret is the convoluted bones of the nose and the unusual internal structure of the nostrils, which contain sacs lined with mucous membrane, a feature the saiga shares with only the whale.

The saiga's nose also gives it an extremely keen sense of smell, in addition to which it has three other physical attributes which have enabled it to survive adverse natural conditions. Firstly, it has excellent eyesight, and, like other animals of the flat, open steppe, it relies mainly on this to spot imminent danger at a distance of 3000 ft (900 m) or more. Secondly, its speed and great stamina can allow it to escape danger. Nowadays the chief adversary is a snowstorm or drought, for its only natural predator, apart from man and the odd steppe eagle, is the wolf, which used to eliminate 20–25 percent of the saiga population until the extermination campaign of the 1950s and 1960s. As the wolf no longer poses much of a threat, the male saiga may live unmolested up to 7 years and the female up to 12.

The saiga's third invaluable attribute is its ability to survive on very little water in the largely waterless steppe and semi-desert. Like the camel, it seldom needs to drink, gaining most of its necessary moisture from the succulent, drought-resistant plants on which it feeds and which, in the cooler season, are heavily covered with early-morning dew and, in the still cooler season, frost or snow.

On the desert island of Barsa Kelmes in the Aral Sea (now a nature reserve) saigas were able to survive, while human beings, fleeing from robber bands on the mainland in the early nineteenth century, died of thirst. Hence the island's name, meaning 'Go there, never to return'. Only during the rutting season in December, when the males are in a highly nervous state and graze little, do they visibly thirst, but then they can quench their need by eating snow.

During this rutting season, while the sexually immature yearling males form bachelor herds, sexually mature saiga males fight each other for the females in battles which can be very fierce and sometimes fatal. Their noses swell and the glands in front of their eyes secrete a strong-smelling, dark-brown substance which enables rival males to identify each other. As polygamous animals, male saigas will attempt to collect a harem, which can be of between 3 and 50 females, depending on their success at discouraging rivals.

The female saiga is extremely fertile and reaches sexual maturity exceptionally fast: 86 percent of females born in the spring will conceive in December of the same year (and 96 percent of the other females conceive each year). In early spring the herds begin to move from their wintering grounds of the warmer, semi-arid south to areas of more abundant vegetation further north. It is here, around the beginning of April, that the males depart, leaving the females to give birth as if in an enormous, albeit scattered, maternity ward of several thousand pregnant saiga. Astonishingly, the females all calve within a week or so of each other. To add to the natural fertility, 75 percent of births are twins, and there are occasional triplets.

For the first day of their lives the baby saigas lie completely motionless on the ground to avoid attracting the attention of any predators and to gather strength. Their mothers, meanwhile, may graze anything up to 2000 ft

(600 m) away, returning towards nightfall to suckle their young. The baby saigas feed on their mother's milk for at least a month, although after only about four days of life they begin to eat steppe grasses as well. After only eight days they are well able to keep up with the adults and can easily outrun a horse.

The saiga is a naturally nomadic and gregarious animal and moves in herds, the size of which can vary enormously, depending on the time of year, from around 50 animals to as many as 200,000. The male–female ratio of herds also varies considerably. The animal's migration patterns are still not fully understood: much depends on climatic conditions and the availability of food, but in general it moves south to warmer, if more arid, areas for the winter and returns north in spring to give birth. Unlike reindeer herds, the migrating saiga do not follow regular paths, because of the variable climate of their habitat. One bad winter may change their route and produce high mortality and, to combat this, nature always provides far more females than males.

Long of commercial importance, the saiga is mentioned in early Kalmyk, Kazakh, Tatar and Mongolian manuscripts. From time immemorial it has been hunted for its meat and hide, but above all for its antlers which, after centuries, are still highly prized in traditional Chinese and South-East Asian medicine. Since the late 1960s, tests in Vladivostok (at the Far Eastern Scientific Centre of the Academy of Sciences) have shown that a preparation from the horn's outer integument, known as saitarin, compares favourably with reserpin's tranquillizing effects and can in addition be used as well as an antispasmodic and anodyne. Perhaps both saitarin and the medicinal plants of the taiga will one day be in use in the West.

Man's demands on the saiga have brought a dramatic decline in its numbers. In the eighteenth century the range of the herds stretched from the Carpathians of eastern Europe to the Altai mountains of south-west Sineria, but by the nineteenth century the western boundary had shrunk in the east to the River Don. In 1733 the pioneering German naturalist P. S. Pallas reported that the Cossacks on the Kirgiz steppe in Central Asia killed saigas with abandon and with no concern that the herds might not be inexhaustible, as with the later slaughter of the bison on the great North American plains.

By 1840 the last saiga in the Ukraine had been killed, and in 1840–50 the merchants of Bukhara and neighbouring Chubinsk alone are recorded as selling 344,474 pairs of saiga antlers. Saigas would often be driven pitilessly onto smooth ice where they were helpless or into barbaric ambushes of sawn reeds which would tear open their stomachs.

The wholesale slaughter continued unchecked until the early part of this century when, as a result of man's persecution, the saiga had stopped its long north-south migration. In 1919 it seemed doomed to extinction but, with only 1000 left, hunting was banned in Russia proper and then four years later in Kazakhstan as well, thus protecting the saiga's residual range. In the next 25 years its numbers rose so rapidly – it can increase by 115 percent each year – that in 1951 licences began to be issued for hunting saiga on a strictly controlled basis (although it is hard to believe that there is no poaching).

Today the saiga may be found only around the northern Caspian Sea and on Barsa Kelmes, but it is the most numerous of the USSR's wild ungulates and its population is stable at more than 3 million. As a result of its extraordinary fertility, some 300,000 head are now culled annually, yielding over 100,000 horns (up to 42,700 are exported each year) as well as hides, fats and 6000 tons of useful meat. The animals are hunted usually at night from a car or truck, the headlights reflecting their eyes, and sometimes shot at the rate of 100–120 in 5–6 hours.

Chingis S. Aitmatov, the famous Kirgiz novelist has written in *The Place of the Skull* (Faber, 1989) of helicopters herding saiga to the point of exhaustion. They were then machine-gunned from vehicles to fulfil the quotas of the meat procurement plan in such huge numbers that it took four days to load them onto containers. Fictional perhaps, but based on fact?

Apart from the culling, there has, according to Boris Komarov's *The Destruction of Nature in the Soviet Union*, been unsought mortality caused by barbed-wire fences around pastures. Thousands of saiga have been killed crashing into them at night at great speed – once, 300 dead were found in only one day on a state farm's fence – and they have also died in irrigation canals. Precautions are now being taken to prevent such incidents.

Nonetheless the overall numbers are immensely healthier than they were. Like the sable, the saiga has been saved from extinction: two endemic species nearly exterminated by man and then rescued only just in time. Now it gallops in its tens of thousands across the steppe and semi-desert.

The early mounted nomads of the steppes such as the Kirgiz have long since been settled and only some semi-nomadic herding remains, attached to state and collective farms. But the old traditions of the steppe are not yet dead in the case of, for instance, the Kalmyks (147,000 in 1979) who live around the mouth of the Volga where it enters the Caspian Sea. Having fled here from western Mongolia in the early seventeenth century, they converted from shamanism to lamaist Buddhism a century later and were deported by Stalin to Siberia in 1943 for alleged collaboration with the Germans who had occupied part of their region.

As one of the traditionally pastoral peoples of the Soviet Union, they based their way of life on the horse, and for centuries they have milked their mares and fermented the milk into koumiss. This fermented mare's milk has an extremely long tradition. According to Theophrastus (371–287 BC), called the father of Greek botany, a semi-nomadic Scythian tribe around the Don could do without either food or drink for 11–12 days if they took liquorice and *hippake*, a cheese made from koumiss. In the early eighteenth century Johann Amman, professor of botany in St Petersburg, wrote that this 'delicate & nourishing substance' was the 'greatest part of their provision' when they went to war or made a long journey through desert countries.

Fifty years later John Grieve, a British doctor who had worked in southern Russia, wrote the first scientific description of koumiss and its medical applications and included case histories of four patients whom he had successfully treated for consumption, debility, digestive disorders and nervous illness. Although Grieve's pioneering work provoked much interest at the time, it was forgotten for nearly a century until 1881, when

George Carrick, physician to the British Embassy in St Petersburg, published book on its uses in pulmonary consumption and other wasting diseases. Carrick even established a koumiss sanatorium in the northern steppes near Orenburg which he called Dzhanetovka after his niece, Janet. (The place still bears the name.) It was a success, attracting many patients, including some from Britain, and Carrick even produced a 'Route map from Great Britain to the Steppes' and brought a demonstration herd of Tatar mares to the International Health Exhibition in London in 1884.

Koumiss is now widely prepared not only in the USSR but in the Middle East, Asia, South America and, above all, Mongolia, and has been found to contain six vitamins including vitamin B complex, 19 amino acids, 800–1000 mg of calcium and various trace elements and active ingredients: one more service the horse performs for man.

That steppe which was once to Gogol 'green-gold ocean splashed with millions of different coloured flowers spurted' may now be cultivated beyond recognition into the Soviet Union's most important agricultural area producing much of its cereal crops, meat and dairy products. In large areas it has changed even more, now highly urbanized and industrialized

For the first day of their lives baby saiga antelope lie completely still on the ground, gathering strength and avoiding predators.

with, for instance, one of the world's largest deposits of iron ore near Kursk and Krivoi Rog and the famous coalfields of the Donbass covering nearly 9,000 square miles (23,000 sq km). Open cast mining has removed the chernozem in many places. Unfortunately, even in the open steppe there are serious environmental problems, just as in the tundra and taiga.

Intensive irrigation has brought the widespread rise of salts to the surface so that in some areas the land is permanently unusable. Pollutants now flow through the chernozem or black-earth region and into the Black Sea, which one Soviet newspaper pronounced 90 percent dead 'in the full sense of the word'. In the Kalmyk steppes, huge herds of sheep, 20 times more than the land can sustain, have created Europe's first desert and continue to graze there. The desert is reported to be spreading by 10 percent a year and is forecast to reach the southern Ukraine in five years.

Unprotected from wind and rain, the vast open fields of European Russia's black-earth belt have lost up to a quarter of their incomparable humus through erosion in the last 25 years, and about 965,000 square miles (2.5 million sq km) – that is, nearly 50 percent of the USSR's agricultural lands – are estimated to be undergoing erosion or under threat. The annual loss to agriculture from erosion (in addition to the ecological and social damage) has doubled over the last two decades to 18–25,000 million roubles. More than 3900 square miles (10,000 sq km) of the nation's agricultural land contains residual DDT (banned but still used in places) at levels above maximum permissible concentrations and 2.2 cubic miles (3.7 cu km) of contaminated water were discharged by agriculture in 1989.

The above figures have been compiled by Soviet officials and published in the IUCN [International Union for the Conservation of Nature] East European Programme's Environmental Status Report 1990. But apart from all these problems in this magnificently fertile area there is that of radiation from the Chernobyl nuclear accident of 1986. As a result of this, 19,300 square miles (50,000 sq km) of Ukrainian farmland have been contaminated, and in August 1990 the Ukrainian Supreme Soviet declared the whole Ukraine an environmental disaster area following Byelorussia's similar declaration.

Unfortunately this is not the only area to suffer radioactive damage. The nuclear tests held for many years in Kazakhstan (and now transferred to Novaya Zemlya) have contaminated grass and soil and, according to Boris Komarov, 'Whole batches of dead saiga have been condemned in . . . [various] cities because of the high radio activity in the meat'. This brings to mind the words of the poet Osip Mandelshtam in the poem on Stalin which was to seal his fate: 'We live, deaf to the land beneath us'. Environmental health presents the gloomiest picture of all, with shortened life expectancy, high infant mortality, congenital defects and respiratory diseases, among other serious problems. We can only hope that the present revolution in the USSR will tackle these difficulties successfully, although it is clear that it will take much time and effort and huge sums of money.

On the very southern edge of the steppe's huge, flat expanse an almost vertical world begins: a range of spectacular mountains with an extraordinary concentration of wildlife. In many ways it is the most fascinating mountain range on earth: Shakespeare's 'frosty Caucasus'.

John Bulmer, cameraman in the Kalmyk steppe

The steppe is a desolate place and it is hard to survive there. There is, though, a scattered community of farmers. Some areas are very, very green and some are saltier than others particularly when below sea level. Other parts are very dry and desolate but in places wild pine grows, giving off a wonderful smell. There are endless Second World War memorials.

There is no specific rainy season and the rain was very random. It was nearly always too hot or too cold. There was so much dew in the mornings; just by tucking in a flap of the hide I could cause rivers of water to run off the roof. My tent was blown flat on the ground two nights in a row. The ground was so hard that the tent pegs would not go in or else it was so soft that they would not stay in. Nothing is in moderation in the steppe.

I was filming the saiga antelope. The saiga is much smaller than a horse, more the size of a goat. We had to film the antelope using the same vehicles the Russians would shoot them from; this proved very difficult as the saiga can run extremely fast, kicking up clouds of dust.

Before the young are born the adults seem to go round in tremendous circles looking for the right place in which to give birth. The females tend to all give birth at the same time, within two or three days of each other. The mothers will give birth and then leave the young, returning to feed them every few hours. At the first sign of a predator the mothers leave the calves lying completely still on the ground.

CHAPTER FIVE

'THE END OF ALL THE EARTH'

... the mountains rose abruptly up out of the distance, a dark, jagged line stretching across the horizon, the giant peaks of the Caucasus; the wall dividing Europe and Asia ...

Lesley Blanch, *The Sabres of Paradise*

These snow-clad giants with their heads in the clouds serve as a barrier against the extreme continental weather systems of the steppe to the north and allow a totally contrasting subtropical vegetation to clothe their south-facing slopes. Stretching more than 900 miles (1450 km) from the Taman peninsula on the Black Sea to the Apsheron peninsula on the Caspian, and including 60 peaks of over 13,000 ft (3960 m), the mountains of the Caucasus and their valleys form a unique variety of climatic systems – and thus habitats – changing from west to east and with almost endless permutations according to altitude, latitude and whether the slopes are north or south-facing. From the eternally snow-capped peaks and the icy world of over 2000 glaciers down to the alpine and subalpine meadows and further down to the forests and orchards of the valleys, the Caucasus embraces a bewildering number of different ecosystems and cultures.

The wild and ancient history of this mountainous meeting point of continents has brought together a remarkable assortment of peoples, plants and animals, and has isolated them from the outside world, often from each other, so that they have developed over the centuries in their own ways.

The mountains are divided into two main ranges – the Great and Lesser Caucasus – which run roughly parallel to each other, north-west to south-

The mountain ranges of the Caucasus combine snow-capped peaks and fertile alpine slopes.

east, with spurs connecting them. The Great Caucasus, the more northerly chain, is in general higher and embraces all the major Caucasian peaks. The highest peaks of the Great Caucasus are twin-peaked Mount Elbruz, 18,345 ft and 18,465 ft (5556 m and 5595 m), and Mount Kazbek, 16,545 ft (5014 m). The Lesser Caucasus is more fragmented and merges into the high plateau of the Armenian highlands to the south. The Great Caucasus range is itself divided into three, the western, central and eastern Caucasus, and, to complete the picture, the western section has several parallel, smaller ranges separated by deep valleys lying between it and the sea.

The Caucasus as a whole forms a link between the low mountains of the Crimea and the giants of the Pamir and Tien Shan ranges of Central Asia, and the many layers and contortions of strata bear witness to the titanic processes that have built its mountains. Geologically these are young, like the Alps, but they are more like the Pyrenees in their general uniformity of orientation and width, which varies from 30 miles (48 km) to 140 miles (225 km).

There are few north–south routes through the mountain wall of the Caucasus. The main routes have always been over the passes of the central Caucasus where the chain is at its narrowest, and even here there are only two passes capable of passage by anything larger than a sure-footed horse or man. One goes through the Daryal gorge and over the Krestovy pass (7800 ft/2365 m); the other is the Mamison pass (9270 ft/2800 m). Through these passes have come innumerable tribes since ancient times. Neolithic and Bronze Age man, Sumerians, Scythians, Sarmatians, and countless others have moved through the Caucasus, leaving some of their number to settle here.

The Greeks called this rich land Colchis, and it was here that Jason and the Argonauts came to seek the Golden Fleece.

'And at day-dawn they looked eastward, and midway between the sea and the sky they saw white snow-peaks hanging, glittering sharp and bright above the clouds. And they knew that they were come to Caucasus, at the end of all the earth.' Thus wrote Charles Kingsley. The myth may indeed have some credence for, traditionally, fleeces were attached to river beds so that alluvial gold dust borne by the current could be trapped. It was here, too, that Medea gathered the magic herbs with which she cast her spell on Jason and his men.

Twice the Romans attempted to conquer the region but were defeated by the ungovernable inhabitants in their impossible terrain. Pliny wrote that one town on the Black Sea's east coast was inhabited by people from 300 tribes speaking so many different languages that 130 interpreters were required.

More and more peoples in time sought refuge in the Caucasus, adding yet more layers to the palimpsest of Christian, Jewish and Muslim settlement and exemplifying the unique scope for isolation offered by this convoluted mountain area.

Perhaps the most intriguing people of all are the Khevsurs, living in remote and almost inaccessible mountain valleys. Reputedly descendants of the Crusaders who perhaps got lost in the region centuries ago, many of them are fair-haired and blue-eyed, and until early this century wore chainmail tunics bearing the Maltese cross which they still wear on special occasions. Nineteenth-century travellers brought back tales of this fiercely independent people with a language akin to Hungarian, who were ostensibly Christian but worshipped St George rather than Christ.

Like the other peoples who have sought havens in the mountains over the centuries, the Khevsurs have remained fiercely independent of their equally inaccessible neighbours until very recent times. Many have now descended from the mountains, although some remain as shepherds in the high places, but even with the gradual coming of roads, electricity and television in many parts of the Caucasus, some 50 languages are still spoken in Georgia (quite apart from Armenia, Azerbaidzhan and Dagestan), their survival resulting from the geographical and cultural isolation enforced by topography.

As such a crossroads of peoples and armies, this great isthmus has suffered a tumultuous history, fought over by Romans, Persians, Mongols, Turks and others. Christianity was brought to Georgia in 330 AD.

In medieval times the Georgians (themselves several related peoples) emerged as masters of the Caucasus. The twelfth and early thirteenth centuries saw the apogee of Georgian culture, particularly under Queen Tamara, but disintegration and invasion were to take their toll over the centuries.

In 1784, therefore, the Georgian king acknowledged Catherine the Great's suzerainty over Georgia, but in the early nineteenth century the fierce and largely Muslim mountain peoples periodically rose against Russian rule, their resistance culminating in the jihad or Holy War waged in the forests and above all in the mountains under their great leader, Shamyl. The nature of the Caucasus and its independent-minded peoples is graphically exemplified by this war.

It took 45 years for a Russian army, which grew to around half a million men, to subdue the mountain tribes, and only then with terrible mortality. Fighting took place in shoulder-high vegetation and dense forests which were alive with enemy sharpshooters, sometimes hidden in giant beech trees with 10-ft (3 m) wide trunks which could shelter 30 to 40 men apiece. One day's long march could take the Russian soldiers from coastal swamps through subtropical forests to mountain passes. In summer they suffered sunstroke, in spring and autumn chill mists and torrential rains, in winter frostbite if they did not freeze to death.

Only by bridging hair-raising chasms could they reach the high plateaux, and only by felling clearings through the forests which hid the enemy – some of the huge beech trees were too big to fell and had to be blown up – could they move their supplies and cannon forward and drive the enemy out. When Shamyl, from the mountains, watched the great trees fall, he knew his cause was doomed.

Thousands of mountain tribespeople were dislodged from their settlements during the Russian conquest of the Caucasus and its aftermath, and in Stalin's time whole tribes such as the Chechens, the Ingushi, the Karachai and the Balkar were deported to Central Asia and Siberia for alleged collaboration with the Germans. Those who survived were allowed to return to their homelands only in the 1950s.

The way of life in the Caucasus has changed over the years. Previously whole families would accompany grazing flocks up to the pastures in the summer months, but today the number of shepherds has dropped considerably.

Other peoples, lucky enough to avoid this fate, such as the Cherkess, Abkhazians, Svans, various Georgian peoples and the Lezghis of Dagestan, have all had their lifestyles eroded to some degree by modernization. Some have descended to work in the towns.

The prolific fruit and vegetables grown chiefly in the central valleys and the coastal plain, and particularly the grapes grown in these parts for thousands of years, have given the local people a deserved reputation for hospitality.

Despite modernization, many of the mountain men still wear the *cherkeska*, the traditional, tightly belted Caucasian coat with rows of cartridge pockets, some silver-trimmed, across the breast, and the indispensable *kinzhal* or dagger in an ornate scabbard hanging from the middle of the belt at the front. Still worn also is the *burka* – a cloak of untrimmed felt, which is water-proof, spear-proof, (almost) bullet-proof and serves as a horse blanket, tent and symbol of virility. When not in use it will stand up in a corner on its own, waiting for its next call to duty.

It is not only the people of the Caucasus who are remarkable for their diversity. The extraordinary variety of mountain, upland and valley to be found, with many different ecosystems resulting, inevitably produces a rich diversity of fauna, much of it endemic. One theory is that millions of years ago, well before the more recent ice ages, the Great Caucasus range was an island surrounded by sea, where animals and plants began to be isolated, and certainly today there is a particularly large number of endemic species of both flora and fauna.

For millennia the Caucasus has served as refuge too for plants and animals. During the ice age, when an ice-sheet covered the mountains down to a level of 3000 ft (910 m) (and even as low as 1200 ft/366 m in some places) all the plant life beneath perished. But in the southern parts of the mountains, beyond the limits of the ice, numerous warmth-loving plants have survived from that time, including species of boxwood (*Buxus colchica*), confined to the extreme west of the Great Caucasus, rhododendron (*Rhododendron caucasicum*) and sweet-bay laurel (*Laurus nobilis*) which grow in profusion on humid western slopes.

Such relict species are inevitably greatly outnumbered by the 6000 species of plant which have developed since the ice age, ranging from mosses to conifers. Each spring the mountain slopes are ablaze with azaleas and rhododendrons, but there are many flowering shrubs, including camellias, lonicera, berberis and jasmine, as well as fruit bushes such as blackcurrant and raspberry, and flowers of all kinds, including campanula, cyclamen and geum – a botanical wonderland.

Rain is one key to such flora, and the western Caucasus certainly owes its rich vegetation largely to its copious rainfall, which is due to westerly winds blowing across the Black Sea. It receives up to 197 in (500 cm), which makes it the wettest place in the Soviet Union. On its southern slopes, sheltered by the mountains from northerly winds, it fosters some 60 species of trees and shrubs. The lower slopes are thus covered with dense broad-leaved and conifer forests, containing an extraordinary variety of flora, including five kinds of oak, two of them native species (*Quercus ponticus* and *Q. sessiliflora*), walnut (*Juglans regia*), two hornbeams (*Carpinus caucasica* and *C. orientalis*) and many varieties of other European deciduous trees. Some trees – particularly the beech and fir – grow to a great age and huge girth, and in many places lianas entwine the tall trees, giving a curiously surreal effect.

In the huge Caucasus Biosphere Nature Reserve there are ancient groves of yew and box. The former grows here to a height of nearly 100 ft (30 m) with a trunk diameter of 6–7 ft (approximately 2 m) by the time it reaches 200–300 years old. Its wood lasts for centuries and rejects most attacks by pests, so it is particularly sought after for carvings, furniture and musical instruments.

The box will live even longer – for 500–600 years – but grows to only about half the height of the yew and a quarter the girth. Boxwood is extremely heavy and will sink in water. For centuries it was used to make shuttles and blocks for high-quality woodcuts, and nowadays it is used to make instrument parts, combs and souvenirs. In the past both yew and box were felled extensively for their valuable commercial use, so that the groves of mature examples of both in the dark and eerie canyon of the Caucasus Reserve's River Khosta are now, alas, unique, and a last reminder of the times when the traders of classical and even earlier times came in search of the precious woods. Yew coffins and furniture have been found well preserved in Egyptian tombs and it is thought that the wood may indeed have come from ancient Colchis.

Above these lower slopes beech predominates and then gives way to thick conifer forests of birch, larch, spruce and pine, including Caucasian species of pine (*Pinus halepensis* and *P. insignis*), and fir (*Abies nordmannia* and *A. orientalis*). Above the thick forest belt the trees become smaller and sparser, and on the subalpine levels above grow rhododendrons and dwarf juniper, interspersed with meadows of long grass and flowering plants: buttercups, delphiniums, ranunculus and other herbaceous plants familiar to the Western eye. Higher still, the alpine meadows are home to shorter grasses and cushion-forming plants: saxifrage, primula and viola.

In the western section of the central Caucasus where the mountain tops run in a continuous crest between Elbruz and Kazbek, all above 10,000 ft (3050 m), many plants grow to enormous size, owing to the unusual humidity and shelter provided by the mountains: grasses 8 ft (2.5 m) high, giant buttercups and larkspur taller than a man and umbellifera (cow parsley and its relatives) with flower heads as big as dinner plates. Rhododendrons grow in such profusion and so close together here that it is difficult to find a passage through. In contrast, on the northern flanks of these mountains the trees and plants are sparser and the land drier. Here the mountains are bare, rock-strewn and dramatic – indeed, almost melodramatic. Gorges give passage to rivers, which, when the snows melt, turn into torrents, carrying all before them out to the northern steppe.

A bewildering variety of orchids is to be found on the hillsides of the Caucasus. Some are common enough, but 13 species are listed in the Soviet Red Book as endangered or rare. These include the bee orchid (*Ophrys apifera*), with its pale-pink petals and reddish-brown lip. Like so many other flowers of the grasslands, this is under threat because of over-grazing by domesticated animals and cultivation of lands which have previously been left undeveloped.

The Caucasian orchid (*Ophrys caucasica*) is endemic to the Caucasus and Dagestan, but is now rare. It has almost spherical smallish roots like clubs and its flower-bearing stem is about 8–14 in (20–35 cm) tall with rosettes of lower leaves. The leaves around the blossoms are yellowy-green with greeny-brown insides. The velvety lip is like a doubled oval and the leaves on the top are shaped like short blades with a heart-shaped central blade. They are reddish dark brown with blue-violet patterns in the form of a letter H.

The fly orchid (*Ophrys oestrifera*), which has pinky lilac upper petals and a dark brown lip is also under threat, as is the Crimean orchid (*Ophrys taurica*), which is also found in the Caucasus. The yellowy-green *Orchis punctulata*, which is found on the borders of the Caucasus, and the *Orchis provincialis*, which has bright yellow blossoms with a slightly darker lip and lemon yellow leaves around the flower, are rare. The purple orchid (*Orchis purpurea*) is slightly more fortunate in that its entry in the Red Book states that while its numbers are limited it is not yet endangered or rare.

Himantoglossum formosum, an orchid which is endemic to the western Caucasus and Daghestan, is not only decorative but useful for medicinal purposes. It is light purple and olive green and grows on the lower slopes of the hills. It is endangered, as is its close cousin *Himantoglossum caprinum*, which is also found in the western Caucasus.

Further east the mountains diminish in height to the Apsheron peninsula and then their structure continues under the Caspian to reappear on the eastern shore in the Kopet-Dag, skirting the north-east frontier of Iran. The gradual slope towards the east is high plateau rather than mountain chain, cut through by deep valleys. As the climate becomes increasingly dry there are fewer trees and coarser grassland and thornbushes.

High on the ridges in the mountains of the Great Caucasus the delicate Apollo butterflies (*Parnassius spp.*) float gently along the craggy slopes and over the bright carpet of flowers – forget-me-nots, buttercups, scabious, primula, geraniums, cornflowers – in the alpine meadows. Another Apollo species – the Black Apollonia (*Parnassius mnemosyne*) – also lives as a relict species on the plains. Here and there occur heavily perfumed golden lilies, eight of them endemic species.

Along the snowline lives the endemic Caucasian snowcock (*Tetraogallus caucasicus*), or snow partridge, which has learned through long evolution to adapt to an extremely harsh mountain environment. As the snowline moves with the season, so the snowcock follows. Its melodious call can be heard everywhere, but it is much more difficult to see than to hear.

The snowcock has an unusual courtship display in which the male pursues the female up and down hill, sometimes flying for short distances but usually running. Both birds frequently give a distinctive whistle, and during pauses in proceedings the male circles the female with his tail fanned out, wings trailing on the ground and his entire plumage puffed up.

A master of evasion, the snowcock will nest only in isolated places. If it is disturbed, it will at first try to run to safety – it flies reluctantly – but if that is not sufficient it will object with loud cries and take off awkwardly down the mountainside, gliding with its wings bent and motionless. The snowcock finds it hard to take off, and heads down the mountainside in a glide, turning to climb and hide behind a ridge. The female nests on the ground, usually in a sheltered place protected by a rock, and normally lays its eggs in April. The snowcock owes its survival in winter to mountain goats and wild boar, which, in their search for food, dig away the snow, revealing wild onions, crocus bulbs and other plants on which it feeds.

The snowcock itself permits other animals to survive, for the wolf, stone marten and magnificent golden eagle, monarch of the heights, are all its predators. So too is man, for its flesh is very tasty. But today it is not so much sportsmen as farmers who are the bird's main human enemies. For, as sheep and cattle pastures spread ever further up the mountain slopes, it is frightened away from its natural habitat. However, as snowcocks still survive in considerable numbers they are not a source of anxiety to conservationists. Nevertheless their habitats are protected in many of the numerous nature reserves now set up in the Caucasus in order to ensure that as many species as possible are allowed to prosper undisturbed by man.

The lammergeier, or bearded vulture, is unusual in that its head and neck are entirely covered in feathers with long black, bristly feathers on either side of its beak. The lammergeier has the unusual habit of dropping large bones from a great height onto rocks below in order to extract the marrow.

The alpine and subalpine meadows are home to a number of birds of prey, including two vultures. Roaming the rocky mountainsides above the timberline is the lammergeier, or bearded vulture (*Gypaetus barbatus*), with a wing-span of up to 8 ft (2.5 m). It eats mostly carrion but occasionally kills live prey such as marmots and even the occasional mountain goat. It uses the same nest for years, which sometimes consists of only a few stones.

The lammergeier lays two eggs in midwinter and the chicks are hatched nearly two months later, in February or March. If both chicks hatch, the younger is killed and eaten by its parents. This huge bird is well known in the folklore of the hill people and there is an old superstition that anyone who kills a lammergeier will himself be dead within 40 days.

The griffon vulture (*Gyps fulvus*), tormentor in Greek legend of Prometheus on his mountain top, is included in the Soviet Red Book of rare and endangered species, but at least thrives in colonies in the high meadows and on the crags of the central Caucasus. It will attack animals as large as an adult tur (*Capra caucasica*), the endemic mountain goat, pinning the hapless animal to the ground and pecking its eyes out with its cruel beak before dispatching and eating it.

One of the larger animals of the Caucasus, the West Caucasian tur, spends much of its time on the rocky heights just below the snowline, particularly in the summer when the mosquitoes and gnats plague the meadowlands. But the lush summer grasses of the alpine meadows tempt the tur back from the heights and in the early morning it descends to graze. If undisturbed it may remain here during the day, but if alarmed will rapidly retreat to the inaccessible places above the meadows. It also descends to the forest levels during the winter in search of food, where the snow is not so deep.

Turs live in groups of about 100 and, while the males like to scale the mountains even as far as the glaciers, the females prefer the lower levels, taking their young into the deep ravines, where they play at fighting by clashing horns. However stupid these animals may appear to be, it is nevertheless impressive to see one standing on some impossible crag, its huge horns outlined against the sky.

The tur has few natural enemies, but many of the young die each year because of cold or other adverse weather conditions. They also frequently perish in spring avalanches.

The Dagestan or East Caucasian tur (*Capra cylindricornis*) is similar to its cousin, the West Caucasian tur, but has rounder horns and, as its name implies, is found in the eastern Caucasus, in the mountains and high plateau of Dagestan. The wild goat (*Hircus aegagrus*), or bezoar, can also be seen occasionally on the heights up to 8000 ft (2420 m), and climbs as high as the snowline from time to time. But the rare Asian muphlon (*Ovis orientalis*) or mountain sheep, an endangered species, prefers the lower slopes, being less skilled than the tur or the goat at rock-climbing. It is one of ten subspecies of wild sheep to be found in the Soviet Union. The argali is endemic in one narrow area and its survival has become a matter for concern. Also listed in the Soviet Red Book is the Caucasian wild goat (*Capra aegagrus* Erxleben). It is at present not deemed to be endangered, but its numbers are fast diminishing.

Another mountaineer is the Caucasian chamois (*Rupicapra rupicapra*), a light and agile antelope which moves about the high mountain ridges as adeptly as the tur, but descends to the forest or finds shelter in caves on hot summer days. These animals also winter in the forest, but otherwise prefer the high, craggy places, despite being easier prey on the open ridges. Overall, their numbers have decreased, largely from hunting, but also because they will not leave their usual locality, even if danger threatens. However, chamois living in the protected areas are maintaining their numbers generally: there are 3000–4000 in the Caucasus Reserve, for example.

Both the chamois and tur, like many other larger mammals and game birds of the Caucasus, have been subject to the attentions of numerous enthusiastic hunters from Western Europe as well as from Russia, seeking heads, horns, antlers and skins as trophies. The local mountain people, too, have long sought items for the pot as a supplement to their usual diet of fat-tailed sheep.

Many a hunting party set forth with local guides into the mountains in search of game. One of the problems of tur-hunting was getting close enough to shoot, and there are frequent descriptions of sportsmen hanging dangerously over a precipice in their efforts to get a pot-shot. Even when they achieved a hit, the tur often either fell to the inaccessible foot of a precipice or retreated to some remote corner of the mountain to die.

One of the many curiosities of the wildlife of the Caucasus is the mountain suslik (*Citellus musicus*), unique to the slopes of Mount Elbruz. This charming little ground squirrel, which lives high on the mountain slopes up to 10,000 ft (3050 m) above sea level, is a variation of the little suslik normally found in the steppes and semi-desert regions.

The imperial eagle (*Aquila heliaca heliaca*), like so many other birds of prey in the Caucasus, hunts the unfortunate suslik, which is an important item in this magnificent bird's diet. They are also fed to the eagle chicks in the nest. There are usually one or two hungry chicks to be fed, but very occasionally three hatch out, and feeding three hungry mouths is a formidable task. The presence of large numbers of susliks in the area helps a good deal in providing enough food for the youngsters. The susliks may spend much of their time standing on their hind legs in order to keep a better watch out for danger, but it does little to prevent many being carried off by their numerous predators. The susliks are carriers of plague, passing on the disease borne by fleas to other animals and occasionally to a human being. Strangely, the mountain susliks on the slopes of Mount Elbruz are free of plague-carrying fleas.

Lower down in the subalpine meadows and on the edges of the forest is found the Caucasian peregrine falcon (*Falco peregrinus*), the goshawk (*Accipiter gentilis*) and the seemingly omnivorous Caucasian buzzard (*Buteo buteo meuetriesi*), which devours jays, woodpeckers and many other birds, hares, voles and forest mice, lizards, grass snakes, locusts and cicadas.

Many of the birds and animals that inhabit the uplands between the snowline and the timberline move up and down the mountain slopes according to the season. The endemic Caucasian black grouse (*Lyrurus mlokosiewiczi*), found along the entire Caucasus, range along the timberline and subalpine meadows in summer, when they eat stalks, flowers and ripening seeds of alpine vegetation, as well as bilberries and strawberries. In winter they descend to the sunny parts of the lower alpine meadow and to the forest to seek shelter and eat catkins, birch and willow buds and the needles of the fir and juniper.

The male black grouse frequently indulges in extravagant displays to assert its territorial rights. When they first arrive on their territories they run up and down the slope with neck stretched upward. Then the breast feathers are puffed up, the head held back, the tail slightly raised, and wings slightly drooped – a stance which reveals the white shoulder patch typical of these birds. They fly upward steeply, then glide, the wings making a whistling noise that can carry about 500 ft (150 m). The white underwings are particularly conspicuous as the bird wheels round and makes spiral movements and even somersaults in the air. This behaviour often becomes contagious and other male grouse will take to the air to impress any female grouse in the vicinity.

In contrast to these territorial displays and general self-advertisement, the courtship behaviour is slightly restrained, increasing in spectacle if more than one female is present. The males closely follow the females, raising and spreading their tails, holding their heads erect and making little jumps. If the female stops, so does the male as he pursues her up and down the slopes until his conquest is complete.

The black grouse nests on the ground in deep cover in rhododendron or other shrub thickets, simply using shallow depressions lined with leaves.

The Caucasian rock partridge (*Alectoris graeca*) too is resident throughout the Caucasus almost to the Iranian border. It likes to range through meadows and particularly favours open woodland where there are juniper bushes. It sometimes moves to mountain forest, and also frequents river valleys and foothills. Its nest, too, is a slight depression in the ground, with a skimpy lining of leaves.

One of the most beautiful birds to be found in the Caucasus is the great rose finch which has deep-rose-coloured plumage with white spots. It is to be found also in the Tien Shan mountains, but the Caucasian variety has a deeper red colouring than its Central Asian cousins. It lives on grassy slopes high in the mountains.

In the valley of the Rioni River and many other lowland areas throughout Georgia and Armenia, there is a resident bird well known in Britain: the pheasant (*Phasianus colchicus*). Legend tells us that this bird, whose name derives from the Phasis, the ancient name for the River Rioni, was introduced into Europe by the Argonauts. The grey partridge too is a familiar sight to British eyes. Living in bushy meadows and fields in the river valleys, particularly in the Kura valley, they are an important game bird, as in Britain.

Karachaev goats browse and forage high up on the mountainside, making use of vegetation such as shrubs and herbs that the sheep do not eat.

Despite appointing lookouts, the mountain suslik, a species endemic to the Caucasus, sometimes falls victim to imperial eagles swooping from above.

The wall-creeper (*Tichodroma muraria*) is a remarkable bird that lives along the steeper slopes of the mountains. With its grey-black wings it is difficult to spot until it flies, when the crimson patches on the wings can be seen. The bird moves along the steep slopes, pressing itself against the surface in search of footholds so that it can extract insects from the cracks with its long bill.

In the mountain meadows and in the woodlands of the Caucasus European bird-watchers would find many familiar birds: woodpeckers, crows, ravens, jackdaws, nuthatches, tits, finches, sparrows, thrushes, blackbirds, robins and wrens.

Among the many smaller mammals of the broad-leafed forests is the stone marten (*Martes foina*), attracted by the plentiful fruits and berries, which it supplements with small rodents and birds. The pine marten (*Martes martes*), in contrast, prefers the coniferous forest for its berries, insects and small animals. Locals claim that the coat of the pine marten in the western Caucasus is the best quality fur in the whole of the Soviet Union.

The long-clawed vole (*Prometheomys schaposhnikovi*), which is endemic to the Caucasus, is up to 6½ in (17 cm) long and has very small eyes and long claws on its front paws. These voles dig complicated systems of shallow burrows in the meadows and excavate plants by the root and drag the whole plant into the burrow, usually without coming out into the open at all. One can recognize the area in which the vole is operating by the numerous 'volehills'. Its cousin, the pine vole (*Pitymys subterraneus*) is common in the subalpine meadows and forest glades, where it provides food for numerous predators. Higher in the mountains lives another relative, the snow vole (*Microtis nivalis*).

The rare Caucasian mink, weasel, numerous species of vole, dormouse, badger and fox are to be found in the western Caucasus, particularly flourishing in the nature reserves. But when one learns of hunting expeditions such as those described by Prince Demidov, who accompanied Grand Duke Sergei Mikhailovich in the Caucasus in 1891, it is perhaps surprising that some species survived at all. Even in those days the Tsar had forbidden the hunting of the increasingly rare European bison or wisent (*Bison bonasus*) which was already becoming rare and had made the slopes of the western Caucasus its last natural stronghold. It was also known as the aurochs, although the true aurochs, a close relative, became extinct in the seventeenth century. Each time the Grand Duke went hunting, he extracted the Tsar's permission to kill three of the beasts. The Grand Duke and his party wounded and killed countless animals and birds, including his full quota of aurochs. One of the trophies is said to be in the Natural History Museum in London. It is scarcely surprising that the European bison exists nowadays only in nature reserves. In 1927, poachers killed the last two survivors.

In 1940 five European bison came to the Caucasus Nature Reserve from Askaniya-Nova. The males had some Caucasian blood in them. For 12 years they were kept under close watch in the Kish Nursery on the reserve, then released, with extra food, into the valley which the European bison had formerly inhabited. Some animals were later transferred to another area of the reserve and set free to roam. They now migrate seasonally within the reserve and breed successfully, having essentially returned to the wild. In 1968 European bison were also introduced into the reserve and a few more added later. This herd has also flourished.

The tur now prospers in several of the nature reserves in the Caucasus, particularly in the Caucasus Reserve, which was founded in 1924 and covers 1017 square miles (2634 sq km) in the western Caucasus, including some of the highest peaks. This reserve nurtures 1500 plant species, including many endemic and relict plants, as well as protecting 192 bird and 59 mammal species.

Another animal whose numbers have fallen sharply from hunting is the European brown bear (*Ursus arctos*), which still inhabits the mountain forests throughout the Caucasus. It makes up for its poor eyesight with its good hearing and acute sense of smell, and its long foreclaws make it an adept tree climber in search of fruit, nuts and acorns. Omnivorous, it prefers a vegetarian diet with a good lacing of honey, and whenever possible raids beehives, despite being stung by the enraged bees. Although it usually moves at a slow, shambling pace, it can move very fast when pursuing prey and enjoys the occasional meal of venison.

During the spring and summer the bears feed on the grasses and umbelliferous plants of the alpine meadows and turn over stones to find beetles, worms and other creatures to supplement their diet. In the late summer and early autumn they descend to the lower levels of the forest, and there they gorge themselves on ripe pears, apples, plums, apricots, peaches, cherries and many other fruits, wild and cultivated.

Occasionally they eat rodents such as the vole, as well as the easily caught fish which teem in mountain rivers. Even young bears quickly learn how to dangle their paws in the cold, clear water and, with a lightning movement, seize a gleaming trout, which they consume tail first, spitting out the head.

Not much is known about how bears choose their mates and how courtship develops. The Russian scientists in the Caucasian reserves are not in general given the resources to do the necessary detailed studies. The bears have not had collars put on them, so it is difficult and time-consuming to track them during the fortnight when the female is on heat in order to study their courtship and mating. One devoted Russian biologist working on a nature reserve in the Caucasus has studied bears for 20 years and has witnessed their mating only twice.

When a female bear comes on heat an interested male bear will follow her at a distance for several days. From time to time she will look over her shoulder to make sure he is still there, but if he approaches too close to her she will snap at him and rebuff him. But later she becomes playful and starts to roll around in the snow. She will allow the male to come closer, and they will sniff each other before wandering off separately again. However, the male continues to follow his prospective mate and she evidently gives him some kind of signal, for when he approaches her again she is ready to mate. After mating, the male bear will spread himself out on the snow and after about ten minutes will pick himself up and return to his normal solitary life, leaving the female to produce and raise her family alone.

In winter the male bear on the southern slopes of the mountains does not normally hibernate, but the female makes a den for herself in which to produce two or three young. In the colder parts of the mountains the male hibernates for two or three months, but by March is on the prowl for food.

Although the bear is protected in the Caucasian nature reserves, in the Caucasus Reserve itself its numbers have fallen to no more than about 200, because many bears leave the reserve to move lower down to the foothills, where they are often killed by hunters.

A conservation success story is that of the elusive deer (*Cervus elaphus maral*) which leaves the protective forest to graze in the summer meadows, returning to the shelter of the forest in autumn to breed. By the 1920s it had been hunted almost to extinction, but its numbers soon began to recover in the nature reserves set up to protect it and other endangered species, in several of which it now lives in considerable numbers. Only in the rutting season, in September and October, does the deer really betray its presence in the forest. Then the stags fight for new candidates for their harems, and loud growls and roars and the clashing of antlers carry through the forest for some distance.

The Kabardino–Bakarsky Reserve and the North Ossetia Reserve are retreats for the wild boar (*Sus scrofa*), another of the larger inhabitants of the mountain forests. In summer it ascends to the meadows, where it ploughs up considerable areas in search of earthworms, bulbs and roots. At other times of the year it prefers to remain in the safety of the woods with their abundant fruits, beech nuts, acorns and chestnuts.

The European brown bear. Outside the protection of the Caucasus Reserve this species is still hunted.

The boar loves to eat willow-herb and in August wherever this plant is in full flower there is a high concentration of boar. When fruit ripens the boar will feed under the trees each night, returning again and again to the same tree as long as the fruit falls. As the fruits ripen, the cherry first and then the pear, the boar will progress from tree to tree. Its habit of returning every night to the same area for its favourite fruit until the supply is exhausted makes it easy to observe the animals feeding, but otherwise the boar is very shy and elusive and so is difficult to find in the wild.

Unfortunately for the boar its tusks and meat made it one of the favourite quarries of the Russian officers in Tsarist days, and it has been hunted ever since. Indeed, over-hunting, coupled with the boar's incapacity to withstand severe winters, has caused its numbers to fall considerably, but it is hoped that with the protection of the reserves it will hold its own.

The beautiful snow leopard (*Panthera uncia*) has all but disappeared from the mountains since 1956, but it is said there are occasional signs of its passing, and that it is even heard from time to time in the remoter corners of the Caucasus Reserve, though there have been no sightings of this rare creature. The lynx (*Lynx lynx*) is also found in that reserve in the forests and high mountain areas. In winter it kills deer and catches birds, and in summer eats voles and other small rodents.

Twenty species of snake are found in the Caucasus, of which only four species are poisonous, among them the Caucasian viper, whose bite is more venomous than the common viper's. Brick-red in colour, and with a black serrated band along the middle of its back, it is often to be glimpsed in the subalpine meadows and forest belt of the Caucasus Reserve.

A snow leopard, one of the rarest of the large cats, is well adapted to the terrain and climate of mountainous altitudes.

The great efforts to preserve the unique natural world of the Caucasus must be applauded. Since 1924 37 nature reserves have been established in the Caucasus, the greatest concentration of them anywhere in the Soviet Union, reflecting the region's great ecological diversity and importance. Fourteen have two or more sections, so in effect there are about 60 reserve areas. Georgia and Azerbaidzhan have 14 nature reserves each, Armenia has five, and others are scattered from the northern slopes of the Caucasus to Dagestan. The most recently established reserve, the Karagelsky–Sevlichsky, stretches across the borders of Azerbaidzhan and Armenia. The reserves embrace every habitat in the Caucasus, from glacier to river valley, with a semi-protected buffer zone round each, where people live and controlled tourism is allowed. There are also areas where licensed hunting is allowed at certain times of year, and, of course, many animals and plants are protected due to the region's very remoteness.

Tony Allen and Chris Catton, cameramen in the Teberda Nature Reserve, Northern Caucasus

The northern Caucasus is very pretty and there is a lot of wildlife there. The scenery is alpine with tall, rugged mountains, alpine meadows, coniferous and deciduous forests, deep river valleys, clear river water. Most of it is totally impassable. There are no roads. To get across from where we were to the other side of the main range 6 miles (10 km) away, we took three bus trips totalling nine hours. There is an ancient silk road that goes near where we were – essentially a horse track, but you couldn't take a vehicle across it.

We sat and watched the wildlife all day as we were waiting for the bears, and we saw a lot: red deer, tur, chamois, bear, grouse, gazelle. Every hour or two, sitting watching a mountainside, we would see something, which, for large animals, is quite unusual.

When we saw a female bear on heat with a male bear, she was walking in front with the male walking behind her, just following. She would give him this little look round over her shoulder to see if he was still there and still behaving himself. We were incredibly lucky. However dedicated you are, you cannot sit for 12 hours a day for the two weeks the animals are likely to be on heat, looking at the opposite valley through binoculars. We must have spent two and a half hours trekking towards one pair, and within half an hour of us getting into position they were mating.

Mount Elbruz from one side is a complete disappointment. The other side is spectacular. There are two steep cliff faces that go up and the glacier comes down and disappears in between them. It's quite dramatic. It's really spectacular to view the surroundings from a helicopter. You see a map of the Soviet Union which is such a vast country that the Caucasus does not look like very much. When we were up above it we realised just how vast the mountain range is. It looks like someone just crumpled up the mountains. As far as the eye can see there is ridge after ridge after ridge. A lot of it is snow-capped, even in July.

There are yak, about 5000 of them now. About 300 yak were introduced from the Altai mountains in about 1982 and their numbers have greatly increased. Yak do not need to have winter fodder cut for them as they can forage for themselves.

Also there are Caucasian black sheep, very good to eat, which are sent to the Kremlin. There are no black sheep anywhere else in the Soviet Union. They are shorn twice a year. None of the fields looked as if they had ever had artificial fertiliser or pesticides. All the sheep meadows are still full of flowers. People do genuinely enjoy their lives there. Up in the mountains we met Mukhtar who was a very happy man. He spent the summer in his hut at about 6560 ft (2000 m) and loved it there.

Up to about 5250–5600 ft (16–1700 m) it was as if we were walking through a European woodland and then we crossed a line at about 5500 ft (1700 m) and went from where we recognised nearly every plant to where we recognised almost nothing. At the lower altitudes we found many plants that in Britain are recognised as ancient woodland species. Things like herb paris, sweet woodruff and lily-of-the-valley are very common there: in Britain they are now rare.

The Caucasian rhododendron is pretty – a pale, creamy white. But there are a lot of very, very colourful flowers. The colours of individual flowers are very vivid. Dots of colour here and there – acres and acres.

There were lots of adders. We walked down one valley and saw five in perhaps 120 yards (100 m). After the fifth we began to wish we had knee-high boots. Although not particularly fond of snakes, we know that they're not a problem and, unless one of us actually trod on one's tail everything is going to be fine, but having seen five in such a short distance, we wonder how many we didn't see and how many tails we almost trod on . . .

CHAPTER SIX

MYRIAD STREAMS, RIVERS AND LAKES

Down from hills and mountains, through steppe, desert, forest and tundra, they flow: nearly three million streams and rivers, draining the huge land mass of the world's largest country. They flow out north into the six seas of the Arctic Ocean, west into the Baltic, south into the Black Sea and east into three seas of the Pacific: eleven seas in all (excluding the Caspian and Aral, technically lakes).

Not only do they affect the climate and govern vegetation and wildlife. For a thousand years and more they have shaped human history, providing sustenance and settlement and natural highways for trade, conquest and exploration. They remain extremely important economically as heavily-used waterways for freight (as well as people), irrigation, electricity and commercial fisheries.

Russia indeed was born on the rivers that start in the unspectacular Valdai hills only 118 miles (190 km) north west of Moscow: the source of the Dvina, Dnieper and Volga. Already in the fourth century Herodotus described the lower Dnieper as 'the most productive river . . . in the whole world, excepting only the Nile . . . It has upon its banks the loveliest and most excellent pasturage for cattle; it contains abundance of the most delicious fish . . . the richest harvests spring up along its course and, where the ground is not sown, the heaviest crops of grass . . .'

It was the Dnieper which saw the rise of Kievan Rus and the baptism of Vladimir, Grand Prince of Kiev, followed by the mass baptism of his subjects in the river (according to legend) and the introduction of Christianity by Byzantine monks arriving up the Dnieper. It was the defeat

Water lilies, lotus and water chestnuts flourish in the avant-delta of the Volga, forming brilliant carpets of colour from mid-June to August.

in 1223 on the Khalka river of a combined Russian-Polovtsian force by a Mongol army which proved the forerunner of Kiev's destruction and the so-called Tatar yoke or subjection to the Mongol empire of almost all the Russian principalities except for Novgorod.

So much of Russia's past is related to its waterways. Novgorod's power and prosperity were due to its location on the Baltic-Black Sea trade route, and once that was severed by the Mongols, it could still maintain its western contacts by water and expand north and east via lake, river and portage. The first victory over the Tatars was the famous battle on the Don in 1380 led by the Grand Prince of Moscow, Dmitry, henceforward Dmitry Donskoy, just as in the previous century Alexander Nevsky, Grand Prince of Vladimir, had first defeated the Swedes on the river Neva, thus gaining *his* name, and going on to rout the Teutonic knights on the ice of Lake Priapus.

Peter the Great chose that same river, the Neva, for his window on the west and he drained its marshes to build Europe's most beautiful capital, St Petersburg, with its multitude of canals. Two hundred years later in the Second World War, under the name of Leningrad, despite nearly one and a half million deaths from starvation, it heroically withstood the Germans' 900-day blockade by the only supply line, the 'route of life' across frozen Lake Ladoga to the north-east. Across the ice came convoys of desperately needed food and supplies, which continued even as the lake began to thaw so that trucks would disappear beneath the surface. The past seems ever present in Russia's lakes and rivers.

Ladoga, the largest lake in Europe at 6834 sq miles (17,700 sq km), teems with a high density of plankton which sustain two endemic fish (smelt and sculpin) and 14 species of whitefish and salmon which all spawn in the lake's rivers. Like Lake Baikal and the Caspian, Ladoga also has one of the world's few freshwater seals (*Phoca hispida ladogensis*). Its population has fallen to somewhere between 5000 and 20,000 due to wolves, foxes and man. Man hunted it for its skin, meat and oil (and erroneously as a predator of valuable fish), but it is now protected, although mass tourism on the lake and Ladoga's industrial pollution are new threats.

Before the Revolution, thousands of Russian pilgrims used to flock each year to the lake's (originally tenth century) monastery on Valaam Island, reputedly one of the most beautiful places in Russia; they might perhaps have continued north-east across Lake Onega, Europe's second largest lake, towards the great Solovetsky monastery, place of pilgrimage in the White Sea. (Onega is now famous for the magnificent old wooden churches on one of its 1650-odd islands, Kizhi; one eighteenth century masterpiece, with its tiers of 22 curved shingled domes, was built without a single nail.)

It was on the banks of the insignificant Moskva, a mere subtributary of the Volga, that a twelfth century *ostrog* or fort arose from which developed the capital of the largest land empire the world has seen and, incidentally, the only capital in Europe to be named after its river. Russia's astonishingly rapid eastward expansion across the north of Asia was primarily due to the river systems of Siberia which necessitated extremely few portages.

Russia's southward expansion also relied on rivers. Catherine the Great sent troops – followed by colonists – down the Volga, Dnieper and Don and, in a campaign based on forts on the river banks, gradually won from

the Crimean Tatars a great new province reaching to the Black Sea and the Caspian. To view her newly-won lands, the Empress and her suite journeyed down the Volga and Dnieper in seven richly-furnished galleys with their own small orchestras and 80 accompanying ships carrying nearly 2000 courtiers and nobles and 3000 troops. Crowds of peasants and Cossacks were drummed up to meet her. To camouflage the poverty and squalor, houses and villages were decorated with wreaths and triumphal arches under the direction of her favourite, Grigory Potemkin, hence the term 'Potemkin villages'.

That famous river, the Volga, on which Catherine the Great cruised in such resplendent style, was to see in the twentieth century the battle of Stalingrad, often considered the turning point of the Second World War, fought on its banks. Hence its post-Stalinist name, Volgograd.

The Volga may be Russia's most famous river and the largest river of European Russia but, at 2194 miles (3531 km), it is only the country's fifth longest and is much shorter than the great rivers east of the Urals: the Ob-Irtysh, 3361 miles (5410 km) long, followed by the Amur, Lena and Yenisei (in that order).

Before 1917, transport was served by only 18,000 miles (29,000 km) of navigable roads in all of Russia – only one hundredth of western Europe's road system. Waterways played the major role in Russia's transportation system, for although the rivers were unnavigable during spring thaw and winter freeze, they were usable for some eight months of the year.

Whooper swans in flight over the Volga delta where they stop to feed during their journey south.

Beaches in the Arctic gulf of the Ob, with its tributary, the Irtysh. The Ob is Russia's longest river and third longest in the world.

As rivers have shaped history, so too have they shaped the landscape and continue to do so even though the flow of many of the largest rivers has been altered by man. The Lena, Volga, and Central Asia's Amu Darya for instance carry tons of clay, silt, rocks and shingle into seas, creating shoals in their courses, and they are constantly enlarging their deltas. During the annual thaw the great pressure of moving ice from the previously frozen rivers gouges the sides of banks and cliffs with consequent subsidence, and in permafrost conditions sometimes reveals the frozen tusks and limbs of mammoths or other animals of the ice age.

Geology, of course, has influenced the immense drainage system from below. Basically, the entire country consists of two colossal tectonic plates, the Russian to the west and the Siberian to the east, with great mountain ranges to the south. In ancient times, the plates alternately rose and fell, covered and uncovered by great inland seas. Indeed, the Caspian, Black and Aral seas were once one enormous linked sea. In the ice age, the ice front blocked Siberia's great Ob and Yenisei rivers, creating vast, swollen water bodies which overflowed into the Caspian and Aral basins. As temperatures gradually warmed, the retreating ice left a chaotic drainage system of extensive marshlands and lakes, which still cover much of the huge west Siberian plain, providing one of the world's largest breeding grounds for waterfowl. Each spring, there is even more water here when the Ob's lower reaches are blocked by ice from the north and enormous floods ensue.

When, each year, the ice on the Ob – sometimes 6 ft (1.83 m) deep – has thawed with its dramatic, primordial breaking, accompanied by a noise as of thundercracks and inexorable destructive strength, fish appear like grayling,

Siberian sturgeon, whitefish and the local speciality, omul or muksun, which in winter is fished through ice holes and eaten raw with garlic, but is now badly affected by the alarmingly high concentrations of toxic oil products dumped in the Ob over the last decade.

The fish, once so plentiful, are now decreasing not just because of the pollution but also because of the wasteful misuse of Ob water. Some of the tributaries of the Irtysh actually dried up completely in 1978, while in others the water level dropped precipitously due to improvident irrigation techniques and over-use by power stations and reservoirs which also resulted in the floodplains around the city of Omsk becoming excessively salty. The loss of precious topsoil and a severe reduction in fish spawning grounds were the unfortunate effects.

Although the world's third longest river, the Ob-Irtysh is only one of the USSR's many great river systems. At least nine others are more than 1000 miles (1600 km) long. Like the Ob-Irtysh, the 2543 mile (4092 km) long Yenisei and 2734 mile (4400 km) long Lena flow north into the Arctic Ocean. The Yenisei, a river Anton Chekhov believed was the most beautiful he had ever seen, forms a clear demarcation between the western Siberian lowland and the central Siberian plateau, by far the two largest geographical entities of the whole country. It flows through what is often an almost impenetrable taiga wilderness of spruce, larch and pine. Sand martins, bitterns, double snipe, and blue doves nest along its banks, and in the taiga can be found the Siberian polecat, sable, bear, wolf and reindeer. Approximately halfway along its course is the Central Siberian Nature Reserve, a magnificent uninhabited area of pristine taiga, crystal clear rivers and fine cliffs where 45 species of mammal, 239 birds and 643 plants are protected.

Some 1100 miles (1770 km) further east, is the Lena, which starts near Lake Baikal and curves its way through the enormous Yakut-Sakha Soviet Socialist Republic (the new name for the Yakut Autonomous Republic), passing at one point the 50 mile (80 km) long 'Lena Columns', vertical limestone cliffs 600 ft (200 m) high, eroded over time into a succession of monumental shapes. Frozen between six and eight months, the level of the Lena rises in May and June, eroding Yakutia's silt, clay, and universal permafrost. In keeping with its other dimensions, the Lena's delta in the tundra of the Arctic coastline is the world's second biggest after the Mississippi, embracing 14,700 sq miles (38,000 sq km) and splitting into 150 or more separate channels. In 1986 a huge nature reserve was established in this delta which protects 29 mammals, 95 birds and 723 plants, 80 more than the ostensibly rich taiga of the Central Siberian Nature Reserve.

Those three rivers are the greatest to flow north into the Arctic Ocean. The longest to flow east into the Pacific is the Amur, exceptionally deep at up to 120 ft (40 m), its basin straddling the USSR, China and Mongolia. Indeed, the Amur and its major tributary the Ussuri form the Chinese border for some distance. Here pressure systems on land and sea converge to create a northern monsoon climate, and the summer and autumn monsoon rains from East Asia, bearing two-thirds of its volume, bring high water of an average 15–18 ft (5–6 m) when the low lying basin resembles a veritable sea. As floods abate, fish can become stranded in small lakes and indeed on dry land, easily caught by hand. In these conditions, the great waterway is even more of a major artery for the population, and water is often the sole means of communication so that the number of boats and motor launches per head of population is greater than on the Volga.

The name Amur may come from a Nivkhi word signifying 'plenty of water', no misnomer in the circumstances (and it has been known to rain on the Amur for more than 20 days on end). The Nivkhi, like the other paleoasiatic peoples of the area, the Nanai and Udegey, have lived around and off the river, fishing and hunting here since pre-recorded time. Descendants of neolithic tribespeople, the Nivkhi are basically fishermen and live in small villages usually on the mouths of spawning rivers.

The Nanai, chiefly fishermen too, fished from birch bark canoes and larger boats about 15 ft (4.6 m) long, made from Siberian pine or 'cedar', and used ingenious trestle systems of willow wicker-work when the fish were coursing the river which funnelled large catches into attached nets.

They chose a good river on which to settle, for the Amur has over 100 species of fish, the highest concentration in any of the country's rivers. It is, too, the only habitat of the kaluga (*Huso clarisus*), a Pacific relative of the Volga beluga sturgeon which can grow to an astounding one ton in weight. Fished to near extinction in the 1950s, these caviar-producing giants are again thriving following a 20 year ban on their fishing and a programme to increase and protect their numbers.

In far greater numbers, however, are the Pacific salmon, famous for navigating great distances from the Pacific Ocean to spawn in the streams of the Amur's tributaries where they were born. They enter the Amur as strong, silver fish and undergo fundamental changes with the transition from salt to fresh water turning finally into a greenish brown to red. Some species acquire a hump from fat deposits, the head elongates and the nose turns into a hooked 'eagle's beak'.

Yet by far the most famous river of the whole country is the 2194 mile long (3531km) Volga. The largest river in all Europe, it drains some 536,000 square miles (1.3 million sq km), flowing south through deciduous and coniferous forests, steppe, and semi-desert into the Caspian. In its basin, the size of France, Germany, Italy and Britain combined, lives one in every four Soviet citizens, nearly 80 million people.

Celebrated in history and folklore, the Volga is very much part of Russian consciousness. A well known song, even more famous abroad, immortalises the Volga boatmen, those peasants – both men and women – who before the steamboat era hauled the laden barges upstream to its chant. At the height of the system there were 300,000 *burlaki*, as they were called, hauling barges from the mouth of the Volga delta upstream to Nizhni Novgorod. It took 70 laborious days to pull a barge those 1200 miles (1931 km).

The Volga is still a major waterway and carries over 50 percent of the Soviet Union's river-borne cargo. It is now the centre of a 70,000 mile (112,650 km) system of natural waterways and canals which connect it to five seas: the Caspian, Black, Baltic, White, and Azov. By the early nineteenth century the Volga had been linked to the Baltic and St Petersburg by three canal systems, and under Stalin an army of slaves laboured, with huge mortality, to construct in 18 months a 63-mile (101 km) canal linking it with the Don.

Since the 1930s, a chain of 12 hydro-electric stations has been built along the river and its tributary, the Kama, and their dams have transformed it into a succession of shallow and slowly draining lakes so that the river's regime is now completely artificial. Where formerly it took the Volga's spring waters 30 days to reach Volgograd from Rybinsk, it now takes nearly 18 months.

The level in the reservoirs is very critical for the turbines, and when the ice – up to 3 ft (1 m) thick – thaws after three months, maintenance must be undertaken. Unfortunately, however, there is little coordination between the Volga's fishing concerns (including fish farming) and the hydroelectric authorities, who halt the river's flow to fix the turbines and cause major floods when they release the water. Fish spawning grounds have been destroyed and 70–80 percent of the fish that survive in the reservoirs are now infected with parasitic worms new to the Volga which kill the fish, whereas, normally, pathogenic organisms and parasite eggs are minimised by a swift river current.

Unfortunately too, there is major pollution. Sewage, pesticides, fertilisers and industrial effluents from the many factories which line the rivers' banks – for example, chemical, metallurgical, machine building and food processing – have had a serious impact at a rapid rate. Ten percent of the Volga's

Traditional traps are still used by some fishermen in the Volga delta.

Carp and bream caught in the avant-delta area of the Volga which runs directly into the Caspian Sea.

OPPOSITE *Fishermen with their catch of sevruga sturgeon, found in the deep water channels of the Volga delta.*

volume is now polluted waste, and in June and July of 1988, unseasonably warm weather combined with industrial pollution to kill millions of fish. In recent years nearly the entire Volga basin has become a zone of ecological disaster.

Yet the Volga still supplies 20 percent of the nation's fish catch, although nearly all fish species have diminished in population and the number of species itself has fallen from 82 to 69. Formerly, several species migrated far up the Volga, including carp, roach, perch, salmon, and sturgeon. Now Volgograd dam, the first above the river's delta, halts them, and shoals of fish mill about its base. Valuable commercial fish, unable to navigate the dams, now have to be maintained entirely by artificial breeding.

Undoubtedly the most famous fish of this most famous of Russia's rivers is the sturgeon. Eight of the world's 16 species of sturgeon are to be found in the

USSR's waters, the others in North America and Europe. In Russia are found the sterlet (*Acipenser sterlata*), the osetr (*Acipenser guldenstadtii*); the sevruga (*Acipenser ruthensis*), and the legendary beluga sturgeon (*Huso huso*), an enormous fish averaging 660 lb (300 kg) and 7–8 ft (2.1–2.4 m) long but which can reach a length of 24 ft (7.3 m) and a maximum recorded weight of 2500 lb (1134 kg). Highly fertile, the female can lay up to 8 million black eggs or roe at one time and live for 100 years or more. Once it was found in most of the major river systems of Europe, and if one was found in the Thames it was considered royal property to be delivered to the crown.

Sturgeons migrate in shoals, some race in autumn, some in spring. Formerly, they travelled 1800 miles (2897 km) upriver from the Caspian to the Volga headwaters, 90 percent spawning there, the rest in the Caspian's other rivers, and because they spawned in two 'shifts', they were able to maximise the Volga's spawning grounds and food resources.

The remarkably interesting sturgeon is one of the most ancient of all fish. Its pedigree goes back at least to the Devonian period (55–60 million years ago) and fossils from the lower Jurassic (70 million years ago). In appearance, it is powerfully-shaped, rather like a shark, and only the sturgeon and shark have a cartilaginous (as opposed to bony) skeleton. Instead of scales, it has 'scutes', long, compact plates of hard skin, which impede its manoeuvrability. Beneath its snout are 'whiskers' which detect food on the bottom, and having discovered them, it drops its mouth down to siphon them in, or lashes food toward its mouth with its tail. When it first hatches, it stays in shallow, well-warmed water, but then moves to the deeper areas of the Volga and the Caspian where it prefers depths of 325–460 ft (100–140 m).

The beluga is the only predator in the sturgeon family, feeding mainly on roach, herring, gobies, anchovies, molluscs, worms and crustaceans. Its intake depends primarily on water temperature, varying from 3 percent of its weight in cold seasons to 21–50 percent at warmer times. With such longevity, its sexual maturity is very late, usually between 14 and 16 years for males, and 19 to 22 for females. When spawning, a great beluga may leap out of the water and fall back with a huge crash. The males fertilize the eggs, which then sink to the bottom and adhere to it, some 120 ft (36 m) below the surface. Fry hatch in less than 2 weeks or, in adverse conditions, nearly 3 months.

The sturgeon has been caught at least since the time of the ancient Greeks, and its meat is not only renowned for its flavour, but for its very high nutritional value; in addition the edible portion of a sturgeon is 80 percent compared to 40–50 percent for most other fish. Large scale sturgeon fishing, however, only began in the eighteenth century and today the fish is caught in the Caspian when swimming near the surface on its way to spawn, by fishermen from fishing stations in the Volga delta. A strong net is let out in a big loop attached to a small fishing boat, and the heaving sturgeon is then hauled back to the boat or bank. Because its size and armour-like skin deprives it of manoeuvrability, it is easily taken, and becomes immobile and passive when caught. Fewer than 100 beluga are now caught each year, they are not killed but stunned and transferred to a special fish barge where the sturgeon are kept alive in fresh water until processing.

A black-crowned heron, which nests in trees, reed beds and low bushes.

Now that migration to their ancestral spawning grounds is blocked by the chain of dams, sturgeon have to be reared artificially in aquaculture pens. Otherwise they would face imminent extinction from the Volga's pollutants; today the eggs of one in three female sturgeons do not hatch at all. Workers now stimulate the males and females with hormone injections to encourage egg and sperm to mature faster, a fact of which the consumer, paying handsomely for the delicacy, is probably quite unaware. In this sad and debatable manner the fish stock is artificially maintained.

More valuable, of course, than the sturgeon itself are its eggs. *The Oxford English Dictionary*'s citation of caviar dates from a statement in 1591, by a traveller to Russia '. . . of cavery, a great quantity is made upon the river Volga', a statement still (at least relatively speaking) true today for the Volga and Caspian provide 90 percent of the world catch of sturgeon and black caviar. Sturgeon, caught in the spring or autumn, are dressed live, since fishermen discovered that egg membranes deteriorate so much in dead fish that they rupture, ruining the egg's solidity and moisture. The roe (15–18 percent of a sturgeon's weight) are scooped out carefully and quickly placed in buckets. Ovaries are rubbed by hand through a sieve screen to remove the pellicles, fibres and fatty matter, washed so each egg is clean, and the roe is divided into different grades according to egg size, colour and fragrance. The eggs are then salted or pasteurised, dry cured or pressed, sometimes even washed in white wine or vinegar and then packed in tins or barrels, with, of course, far more 'pink' caviar than black.

Cattle in a flooded meadow or poloya. Formed by spring or autumnal flooding, the level of a poloya drops progressively through the summer months, yet provides a fertile spawning ground for fish.

The colour of the eggs reflects the species and ranges from the black or very dark grey of the beluga to a yellow tinged grey-brown of the osetr sturgeon. The different colours have traditionally denoted the quality of caviar – and an ancient Greek saying, 'he sold him on green caviar', indicated deception and non-existence.

The USSR now exports an average 100 tons a year of its estimated 1000 ton production (3.5 to 4 tons of it to Great Britain), and this brings essential foreign currency to the state – and to the black market. Despite restrictions on sturgeon fishing, well-armed poaching groups travel the waters in search of the spawning fish (which are located near the surface). The black market price is now more than one pound sterling for one gramme (0.04 oz) of beluga caviar, and hotel waiters in the big tourist cities now discreetly offer black market caviar (not on the menu) to foreigners for large prices for a small jar or tin. Ordinary Russians travelling abroad can have their luggage searched to see if they are exporting caviar.

Despite the decline of the sturgeon and the Volga's problems, the Volga delta probably teems with more wildlife than anywhere else in the whole country. This is, indeed, one of the most dynamic deltas in the world. It begins just north of Astrakhan, about 47 miles (75 km) from the Caspian in a region of sandy, ridged dunes, where the reduced river's interweaving channels below the Volgograd dam branch out into many more channels and shallow floodplain lakes, and then finally into 500 channels, rivulets and 'kultuks' or irregular bays.

'Poloyas' (temporary bodies of water formed by spring and autumnal floods) begin in the shallow floodplains and channels, stretching almost to the delta's edge. Although the Caspian has been rising over the past decade, its level has dropped and the delta greatly advanced into the sea, primarily due to water diversions from the Volga. Five different areas comprise this remarkable delta: the avant-delta directly adjoining the Caspian; the kultuk zone, dotted by sandbars; the forest zone consisting mainly of willow forests; the bulrush-reed bed zone; and the 'solonchak' meadows overgrown with bulrush, tamarisk shrubs and Caucasian dewberry.

The delta supports a multitude of plankton, vegetation, birds, fish and mammals. The profuse aquatic plant life includes yellow water lilies, salvinia, Caspian lotus, and water chestnut. This last grows a nut with two hornlike projections, which is eaten by geese, boar, water voles and other animals, and by humans either raw, roasted like sweet chestnuts, boiled, or milled into a tasty flour. These nuts are used also for animal feed and two and a half acres (1 hectare) alone can yield around 4400 lb (2000 kg) of nuts.

Great 'carpets' of Caspian lotus blossom appear from mid-June to August, changing from a deep pink to almost white, and sometimes extend across 150 acres (60 hectares), their fruit receptacle hiding edible seeds and with leaves which can grow to 30 in (80 cm) in diameter.

In the shallow water flourishes long thin green tape grass which provides important concealment for fish from predators, but which nonetheless nourishes many duck and swan colonies on their long migratory journeys to and from the taiga and tundra.

To the bird watcher, the delta is a paradise on earth. Everywhere there is the incessant sound and movement of birds; their voices can be heard a mile and a half (2.4 km) away as a continuous low pitched roar. Swans, geese, ducks, herons, terns, ibis, egrets, cormorants, pelicans and other species are here by the thousands. The ducks here – mallards, pintails, widgeons, gadwalls, teal, tufted, gargany, dabbling and grey ducks – plus the geese and swans, are estimated at an astounding 5–7 million birds per season.

It is the nutrients in the water combined with the abundance of vegetation which attracts these huge numbers. Nearly 230 bird species frequent the delta, either nesting, wintering, or resting from flight. Forty-eight of them are waterfowl, nesting in willow trees, bushes, or reeds in the lower reaches of the delta. Half of the birds fly from the Arctic regions, and the rest originate in Europe, Mongolia, China, or the Mediterranean. What attracts them in these huge numbers is the concentration of fish, nutrients and plants, the relatively undisturbed location, and the voluminous flow of fresh water despite the Volga's dams.

Colonies of terns, laughing and great black headed gulls make nests on floating tape grass, lilies, salvinia, and other water plants collected and brought up by foraging coots. Broken bulrush reeds supply abundant nesting material for greylag geese, whooper swans and – surprising to find in the USSR – two rare pelican species, whose incessant hooting can be heard over great distances: two to seven nesting pairs of the eastern white pelican (*Pelecanus onocrotalus*), total USSR population 7–9000, and 160 nesting pairs of the Dalmatian pelican (*Pelecanus crispus*) with much the same USSR total.

Pelicans are particularly sensitive to territorial intrusions which can threaten nestlings, which are born completely helpless, bare and blind, only learning to fly at three months of age. They nest in secluded sites near the 'kultuk' and large sections of open water, their choice of nesting areas limited by poor diving ability inherent in their ultra-light bone structure. In these areas the pelicans build a 'nesting raft', with one nest adjoining the next, building several hundred nests in one season. To encourage the two pelican species, biologists in the delta's nature reserves have built additional rafts of reeds, but pesticides and decreased water flow in the delta have sharply reduced their habitat, and their survival is tenuous.

In the white willow forests, intricate woven nests hang above the water, constructed by the penduline tits (*Remiz pendulinus*) from silky willow seeds. In these forests nest cormorants, egrets, herons, spoonbills, and ibises. Cormorants always occupy the white willow forest's edge, in heaped nests of twigs and reeds on the river channels, as their 'straight line' flying prevents them manoeuvring in dense vegetation. The cormorants play an important role in the delta's ecosystem, depositing a large quantity of minerals from their excrement and organic matter such as dead nestlings or eggs.

Egrets and herons (together numbering more than 21,900 breeding pairs) live in broad, flat nests high in the willow trees away from the water's edge. When stalking fish, frogs, or insects, on their stilt-like legs, they keep clear of the water or risk becoming waterlogged and drowning. They feed in shallow water, holding their bodies horizontally, stalking slowly, then stopping and stabbing downwards, or waiting for prey to come within striking distance.

Herons may build up to 50 nests in a tree, although the average is four or five. Their plumes and postures play an important role in identifying the right species to court. Courtship consists of displays, and preening their mates' feathers to cement a pair's bond (and deal with fleas and lice).

The spoonbill's nest is distinguished from the egret and heron nests by a crown of green branches. The spoonbill flies in circles above the colonies, and its odd style of flight makes it seem to fly with its feet forward. All these species continue to nest for many years in the same forests, and one willow tree in an old colony may have five or six nests of different birds.

Carrion crows and ravens are intelligent and wily predators of their fellow birds. They settle among heron colonies and if herons fly from their nests for any reason, they drag out and eat the nestlings or eggs. Scientifically speaking, this is kleptoparasitism, an opportunistic form of pirate feeding, which occurs in areas of large amounts of food. Scientists in the delta have to be wary with their research work, in order not to disturb the herons and give ravens or crows greater opportunity to raid the nests.

The delta's huge bird colonies also support terrestrial life such as wild boar, the only hoofed mammal in the nature reserves, and found from the delta to the avant-delta. Its fresh scat and beds are seen everywhere, and it provides some of the only paths available to man through the thick vegetation. Boars scavenge the remains of fish brought to the nestlings or washed up on the shores. Although spoilt in this respect, every six to eight years the delta experiences high winds and strong floods, and then many boars die from hunger, exhaustion, and hypothermia as the water

As winter approaches, the water lotus begin to droop and wither, yet still provide a marvellous spectacle of aquatic plant life.

A penduline tit at its nest, intricately woven from silky willow seeds, with a small cylindrical entrance at the top.

submerges the islands and sandbars. To save the animals on such occasions, the nature reserve workers and others build earthen embankments and small hills on which they deposit survival rations. Winter in the delta, too, is a difficult period. Ice floes and rising water worsen feeding conditions so that boars, minks, racoons and others may die in search of food.

Teeming with so many birds and some 30 species of mammals, the Volga delta should be a naturalist's paradise. But from June onwards a host of predatory insects descends: 48 species of mosquitoes alone, with another 52 species of midges and horseflies in search of sustenance are a wonderful food supply for birds and fish and an important part of the delta's ecology.

Underwater, the delta is host to 61 species of fish and it has been a traditional fishing ground for centuries. Within its nature reserves, the most numerous fish are carp and the extraordinary catfish. When high water begins, the catfish moves from deeper channels into the 'poloyas' to spawn, the female somersaults dramatically over the male, simultaneously shedding her eggs (icthyologists believe the force of the somersault loosens the roe, readying them for dispersal). Both males and females move the eggs to nearby grass, where they are 'sat on' by the male for several days.

One of the most valuable commercial species of fish in the delta is the roach (*Rutilus rutilus*) which lives in fresh water and fresh water influx of the Caspian, but has, interestingly, adapted to salt water. It has also changed its feeding habits to feed on molluscs and, swimming in large shoals, is easy prey for fish-eating birds and fishermen, and a vital link in the delta's complex food chain. Shoals of herring and shad are also numerous, but the famous sturgeon and salmon merely pass through the delta (if not caught by the fishfarmers) in an effort to spawn up the Volga.

In the spring, when the Volga's water level rises, hundreds of frogs spawn on the water meadows, often becoming prey for grass snakes in the process.

This enormous delta with its abundant fresh water teeming with nutrients, flora, fauna and, above all, the colossal numbers of birds, is perhaps ecologically the richest habitat in the entire country. Yet, unfortunately, there are serious and longterm threats to its health and the health of the whole Volga basin. Hydrocarbons, such as phenols, escaping from the Volga's many petrochemical and metallurgical industries, are present in the water and the vegetation. Synthetic detergents from domestic wastewater are five to ten times higher in the Volga than in the Rhine and other European waterways. Crustaceans and molluscs (excellent indicators of pollution as they strain the water for plankton) contain heavy metals (such as zinc, nickel, cadmium, copper, and lead) which are believed to contribute heavily to the gradual disintegration of the water's life forms. The liberal application of agro-chemicals in the Volga basin's vast farming lands drains ultimately into the main body of the river and pesticides have been detected in muscle samples of wild boar, mink, racoon, carp and pike.

Yet for all its size, fame and wealth of wildlife, the Volga is merely one tributary, albeit the largest tributary, of the Caspian Sea, producing 80 percent of the sea's fresh water, the rest being supplied by smaller rivers, atmospheric precipitation and subterranean springs. Technically, the Caspian is the largest lake in the world, 168,000 sq miles (371,000 sq km) in size and its basin drains more than half the European USSR.

Lying 92 ft (28 m) below sea level, the Caspian is unique as a huge water body receiving rivers with no outlet to the world's oceans. While nearly 25 million acres (100 million hectares) of adjacent territory, mainly to the north and west, supply 30 percent of the nation's fish and crops, its eastern shores are harsh desert stretches, dotted by salt marshes and saline lakes, in years

The town of Astrakhan lies on the banks of the River Volga which carries over fifty percent of the Soviet Union's substantial river cargo.

past the domain of Kirgiz, Turkomen, Kazakh, and Karakalpak nomads.

Man's effect on the Caspian and its basin is pronounced. For more than 30 years a complex of oil rigs has stood in the southern Caspian off Baku, and the water contains oil pollutants and metals, pesticides, fertilizers and waste. Since the introduction of the Volga's dams the level of the sea has dropped correspondingly, and the shallowest and most productive section in the north Caspian has shrunk by 25 percent since the 1930s.

The Caspian's problems, however, are nothing compared to those of the Aral Sea, some 300 miles (480 km) to the east in the middle of Soviet Central Asia's huge desert region. These have been labelled by the Soviet press with little exaggeration as 'one of the very greatest ecological problems of our century'. The Aral has existed for 35 million years, and has undergone drastic change in the last 10,000 years. Man's relatively recent contact with the Aral began perhaps with Genghis Khan's campaigns, when the Mongols lowered its level by damming one of its great tributaries, the Amu Darya. In the past the sea has always replenished itself naturally but, since the late 1960s, it has faced the gravest challenge to its survival.

Its two sole tributaries, the great Amu Darya and Syr Darya, have been used for irrigation across millennia, but from the 1960s a major expansion of irrigation virtually doubled the water extracted (primarily for the mono-culture crop of cotton). At times, half the rivers' flow was used for irrigation, and for 12 years the Syr Darya did not reach the Aral Sea at all. The Amu Darya failed similarly for five years.

The result was that between 1960 and 1987, according to Philip Micklin, the US expert on the question, the Aral dropped from fourth to sixth place among the world's lakes; in that time, its area fell by 40 percent, its volume

During the breeding season little egrets develop the long, distinctive plumage that covers the base of the neck and the back.

by 66 percent, its level by 43 ft (13 m), and its average depth by 21 ft (7 m). In thirty years it has shrunk from 25,675 sq miles (66,500 sq km) to 14,090 sq miles (36,500 sq km) and its shores have receded by up to 50 miles (80 km). Vast areas of its bed have now totally dried up, exposing huge amounts of salt which make any revegetation extremely difficult; many major salt sandstorms have occurred (29 indeed by 1981). They were first noticed by Soviet cosmonauts and now seem to be increasing in frequency and scale with enormous quantities of wind-blown salt deposited each year over a very extensive area.

Looking back to the 'conquest of nature' era, a centrally conceived plan by Moscow water experts in the 1960s actually sought to drain the sea for the irrigation of cotton fields by 1980, after which re-directed Siberian rivers were to provide Central Asia's water needs. Scientists claimed that a decrease in the Aral Sea – or even its disappearance – would have no negative effect upon the climate, the surrounding environment, or the people who lived there. Moreover, in the 1970s, a map was made by planners at the Soviet Academy of Sciences, which shows rice was to be grown in vast quantities on the dried up sea bed.

The projected Siberian river diversion scheme is a classic example of man's until recently unchallenged belief in his right to meddle with nature with impunity. Plans were developed in the early 1970s for a gargantuan multi-million rouble system of dams and canals. These would divert water from the north-flowing rivers, Ob and Irtysh, flowing 'wastefully' in the Arctic Ocean, south instead to the parched republics of Central Asia. the 'project of the century' was slated to begin in the late 1980s or early 1990s, but was halted largely by scientific protest and attacked in the Soviet media for its unfeasibility, huge cost and enormous environmental damage. Water experts advised that the astronomical sums would be better put to use in existing irrigation systems in the Aral Sea region (which has yet to happen). As it is, the amount of water actually used to irrigate the fields in Central Asia exceeds by two or three times the norms recommended by specialists.

In this way, Siberia's rivers were to be diverted to solve Central Asia's water problems. In 1986, however, the Soviet government decreed a halt in construction and further planning. Yet such is the calamitous situation of the Aral and the surrounding population that the Central Asian authorities continue to press for the Siberian river diversion scheme as the best solution to the problem.

The drop in the Aral's level of 42 ft (12.7 m) in 27 years has led to higher salinity for the remaining water as well as the salinization of the surrounding land, vast tracts of which are now salty desert. The resulting climatic changes only serve to perpetuate the vicious cycle. Along with salt, wind-blown soil contains dangerous residues of pesticides, herbicides, and defoliants (chief among them DDT and Agent Orange) from tilled land, used to meet higher production targets. These have become concentrated in the sea, by winds, and sucked up into the atmosphere, entering drinking water and the food chain and are carried vast distances in the heavy wind-blown dust of the desert. The effect on the region's 30 million population is incalculable. Visitors to the only hotel in Aralsk are advised water is available only in the morning and late at night, and the taste of salt is on the

Most cormorants live and breed in colonies. The waters beside the extensive reed beds of Phragmites *provide an ideal feeding ground for the cormorants during their time in the delta.*

lips and skin. Ninety percent of the local women suffer from anaemia, tuberculosis is common, and breast milk is of poor quality. In some areas, infant mortality is 100 per 1000 births, congenital deformities and mental retardation in children have become increasingly common, and deaths from hepatitis have doubled in the last decade.

Wildlife has suffered no less; of the Aral region's 173 original animal species, only 38 now survive, and of the many fish species in the sea itself, there is no trace left. In the 1950s the Aral produced 40–50 tons yearly of sturgeon, pike and roach; now there is no fishing harvest and all 24 endemic fish are extinct. The big fish canneries at what were once ports have reduced their workers and in order to survive are canning fish brought at great expense from far-off seas and the 60,000-odd people formerly involved in the Aral's fisheries must look elsewhere for work in a desert area.

In March 1991, the USSR Supreme Soviet declared the Aral Sea to be an ecological disaster area, and appealed to UNEP (United Nations Environmental Programme) for help. They also declared the bulk of the responsibility for saving the sea was to be borne by the riparian republics. An inter-republic Aral Sea commission was set up to reform agricultural practices and irrigation and develop a child health programme.

The task is an awesome one, and the Central Asian republics, among the poorest in the Soviet Union, are struggling against Soviet bureaucracy, local vested interests, and the sheer enormity of the problem. Even Genghis Khan was unable to wreak such havoc upon the earth.

Two thousand miles (3220 km) north-east of the Aral sea, further east than Singapore, is the most remarkable lake not just of the USSR but of the whole world, with the added bonus that it is set in magnificent taiga-clad mountain scenery almost empty of population. Lake Baikal is by far the deepest lake in the world, an ancient rift valley with a maximum depth of 5370 ft (1637 m), and there is some evidence that it has been even deeper. Its great depth and surface area combine to produce the world's largest freshwater reservoir containing more than a fifth of the planet's supply. More than 330 rivers and streams enter the lake, but there is only one outflow, the Angara.

Baikal is also the world's oldest lake, dating back at least 25 million years, compared to about 20–30,000 years for almost all other lakes on the planet. Those millions of years have provided a unique opportunity for very many species to evolve here in isolation. The result is by far the greatest concentration of endemic species in the Soviet Union and infinitely more than in any other lake on earth.

Of the 1550 animals and 1085 plant species and subspecies in this great body of water some two-thirds are found nowhere else on earth. The largest inhabitant is the Baikal seal (*Phoca sibirica*), endemic to the lake but closely related to the seal of the Caspian. Silvery grey in colour with a yellowish-white belly, this is the smallest of all seals, up to 5.4 ft (1.65 m) long and 286 lb (130 kg) in weight. There are around 70,000 of them, and they particularly congregate on the steep and remote Ushkany islands. In general they are extremely shy and seldom seen except on the ice in winter (which can last for five months) where they bear their pups in February and March, and where a fixed quota is shot by professional hunters from local

enterprises. Baikal seals have indeed been hunted since at least the eighteenth century for their skins, fat and meat.

Greylag geese, timid birds which graze in flocks and fly in skeins.

The seals are believed to have migrated to Baikal in the ice age up the river systems from the Arctic Ocean and it is thought that the omul (*Coregonus autumnalis migratorius*) did the same. One of the lake's 52 species of fish of 12 families, the endemic omul is the great delicacy of Baikal and has constituted nearly three-quarters of the lake's commercial fish catch. Unfortunately, overfishing and pollution have reduced its numbers, size and growth rate, and for a long time its commercial fishing was banned. Now 8–10 percent of its population has to be bred artificially.

Baikal has its own sturgeon (*Acipenser baeri baicalensis*), now rapidly declining despite a ban on its fishing since 1947. But its most remarkable fish is the endemic golomyanka (*Comephorus baicalensis* and *C. dybowskii*), the sole representative not only of a genus (*Comephorus*) but of a family (*Comephoridae*). Up to about 6 in (15 cm) long, the golomyanka is almost transparent and, with no swim bladder, can sustain the enormous difference of pressure between the surface waters and the great depths. The female, moreover, does not produce eggs but 2–3000 living fry.

Perhaps what excites evolutionary scientists more than anything else at Baikal is its extraordinary number of gammarids or freshwater shrimps. One-third of the world's total is here: 225 species of 35 genera, and all but one genus is endemic. The bottom-dwellers have no eye pigmentation but exceptionally long antennae to feel their way in the darkness.

One gammarid plays an important part in the lake's complex self-purification system: the tiny, 0.08 in (2 mm) long *Epishura baicalensis*. Here in incalculable numbers of millions, this tiny creature consumes algae and filters bacteria from Baikal's upper layers, so contributing to the famous purity of this enormous volume of water.

Alas, the purity is now not all that it was, although the main problems are confined to specific areas and all looks pristine nature to the casual visitor. Industry is the chief culprit, above all the huge pulp and cellulose combine at Baikalsk on the south coast which was built in 1966 despite much opposition. The continuous and massive discharge of (at first, totally untreated) effluence into what is regarded as the 'Pearl of Siberia' has produced sustained environmental lobbying and adverse publicity ever since (even in the pre-glasnost days). Now, despite the installation of extremely costly purification equipment, the plant is discharging nearly 523,000 cu yards (400,000 cu m) of inadequately treated waste a day, and life in the water around has changed. For years there have been plans to convert the combine to other uses to end the effluence, but nothing is yet finalised.

A second, smaller pulp mill at Selenginsk on Baikal's largest tributary, the Selenga river, has now been converted to a closed-cycle system, but it and the effluence from the city of Ulan-Ude up-river have badly hit the chief spawning grounds for some of the lake's endemic fish, including the omul. There are also the problems of fertilizers and pesticides, waste oil products, logging operations and air pollution from Baikalsk and nearby industries. The new town of Severobaikalsk on the northwestern coastline is adding to air and water pollution.

But there are signs of hope. Local people feel very strongly about their lake and several pressure groups have been formed, among them the Baikal Fund. The powerful USSR Academy of Sciences' Siberian Department is backing two new international research centres on either side of the lake which will involve foreign scientists and experts, and Baikal is likely to be nominated by UNESCO as a World Heritage Site which will give important protection. The problems of the Aral Sea and Lake Baikal are the two best known environmental issues relating to the USSR's water bodies, although many other lakes (including Ladoga) and inland seas have their own, less publicised, problems. There are also the artificial 'seas', as the country's largest reservoirs are justifiably called. The Bratsk Sea, for instance, on Siberia's dammed Angara river, tributary of the Yenisei, covers 2110 sq miles (5470 sq km), and powers what was the largest hydroelectric station in the world when completed in the 1960s, superseded since at Krasnoyarsk on the Yenisei.

These, of course, are only two of the many hydroelectric projects which began to fulfil the cry of *electrifikatsiya* in order to industrialize the Soviet state. They have, of course, greatly helped the economy, but there now exists what is known as the 'reservoir problem'. Not only have fish suffered badly as in the case of the Volga. Flooding across the country, much of it of agricultural land, has dislocated a sizeable human and wildlife population and submerged huge areas of fertile soil, grazing lands, and valuable forests, in some cases felled but never removed. In some places the local climate has changed for the worse, in some the surrounding land has become

Farmers on the Volga delta set farmland and reeds alight to clear the terrain; this can endanger bird life if the fire spreads into wooded areas.

waterlogged. Shallow reservoirs in summer can warm to a point where algae bloom profusely, eliminating oxygen and thus fish.

As for the rivers, the Volga is certainly not the only one to have problems. Pesticides, fertilizer, raw or semi-treated sewage, industrial wastes, some of them toxic, badly pollute all too many rivers and kill, or at best degrade, wildlife. According to the report of Goskompriroda (the USSR State Committee for the Protection of Nature) for 1989, the USSR's waterways received 200,000 million cubic yards (153,000 million cubic m) of waste water, of which 43,000 million cubic yards (32,600 million cu m) was polluted. These waste waters 'brought more than 40 million tons of pollutants to watersheds and waterways', including 21 million tons of sulphates, 19 million tons of chlorides, 74,000 tons of oil products (much of them doubtless from oil spills) and presumably some of the 255,000 tons of pesticides and 25 million tons and more of mineral fertilizers used by agriculture in 1989. The report cites the Volga, Dnieper, Neva, and Kuban (north of the Caucasus) as the worst affected rivers and names the worst water polluters as the wood, pulp, and paper industry, followed by the petroleum and petrochemical industry.

The water quality has damaged the population's health (particularly in the Aral Sea area), and to this the Chernobyl nuclear accident has added its own severe problems. Quite apart from all the other enormous difficulties posed by the accident including the evacuation of at least 138,000 people and the contamination of more than 4050 sq miles (10,500 sq km), there has been the almost insuperable problem of water contamination. Some areas were thoroughly washed down to decontaminate them, but where could the water flow to but ultimately into the rivers? And what about subsequent rainfall and melting snow? As an emergency measure, 12.4 miles (20 km) of dikes were constructed to prevent radiated water reaching Kiev's reservoir but they can hardly have been built overnight. Fishing was banned on the Dnieper, Pripyat, and Sozh rivers, but the huge contaminated area embraces the Pripyat marshland frequented by migrating fowl, and many of these birds have undoubtedly been shot and eaten.

The fish catch in all major rivers and lakes is declining, and those fish that are actually caught are often weak and diseased. It is estimated that 700 times more petroleum products than is the permissible norm exists in the nation's water systems. Many rivers are also polluted with mineral fertilizers and pesticides, so that fish suffer from diseased muscles or their livers fail to function and they die. In 1989, 70 percent of all fish in the Volga's reservoirs contained mercury.

Water, already a health hazard in many areas, is also becoming a political and inter-ethnic hazard in Central Asia, where its scarcity is increasing national and political tensions. Water disputes between Uzbeks and Turkmens have apparently resulted in raiding parties blowing up each others' canals and pumping stations on the Amu Darya and Syr Darya. The Kirgiz and Tadzhik republics are now reported to want to charge other republics for their use of their water.

But despite the sadly numerous environmental problems, the picture is by no means all bleak, and the vast landscape still holds many rivers and lakes as clear as crystal where nature's cycle is as it has been for millenia.

Tony Bomford, cameraman in the Volga delta

Birdlife depends entirely on the time of year. In the autumn, sitting in a hide, I saw one of the highest concentrations of birds I've ever seen anywhere with 2–3000 birds gradually drifting in. Occasionally, a sea eagle would fly over and panic the flocks. The eagle, besides feeding on fish caught by the cormorants, tests the ducks, geese and swans, looking for a weak link. For instance, some birds may be injured, wounded by hunters with the wound going septic within days, or they suffer from lead toxicity. As the eagles fly over the flocks, the fit birds rise quickly and it is the last ones to rise in which the eagles are most interested. Occasionally, they will whiffle sideways and snatch a bird or nestling.

With such huge numbers of accessible fish, there are plenty of fish-eating birds including vast cormorant colonies during autumnal roosts. In places the sky can be literally black with cormorants. They have quite a dramatic display of breeding plumage, with a stiff, upright crest on the head. When they pick a nest site, the unattached birds will flap their wings to display white spots beneath their thighs. They are flashing a sort of morse code to lure prospective mates into the nest.

The eagles harry the cormorants. It gets significantly colder in autumn in the eastern delta and eagles move westward through it, going from Obzhorova then Trekhizbinka, concentrating in Damchik. You can see 12 or 14 white-tailed eagles in the sky at once – perhaps the greatest concentration anywhere on earth. They work the cormorant roosts and although perfectly capable of fishing for themselves, or even taking a cormorant, they prefer to harry the cormorants, simply circling close to the willow trees, so that the cormorants get scared and fly off. To lighten the load, the cormorants regurgitate their last meal of roach into the river, and as it floats on the open water, the eagles dive for the partly digested fish. The eagles remain until the water freezes over, then, travelling to the edge of the ice, they prey on Caspian seals which pup on the ice, and may scavenge on dead seal pups. It is dramatic to see the eagles talon-grappling; one eagle flies along and another above it, and the one below turns on to its back, the two lock talons briefly, then part and fly off. Some of it is courtship, some of it is

play, done between adults and juveniles and combinations thereof.

In the upper half of the delta are great rook colonies. I was really excited by the red-footed falcons in amongst the rooks. They breed in unused rook nests and live perfectly happily with the rooks. This was the first time I had seen these birds in large numbers, and the falcons flew above our launch every excitedly.

Continuing down the delta, you leave the willow area and enter the 'poloyas' or flooded meadows. Normally during the second half of April vast areas are covered by shallow water with few trees virtually all willow, the predominant tree here, and they continue in clumps wherever there are patches of land which are sometimes dry. Beyond that are acres and acres of reed-bed, maybe 15–20 ft (4.5–6 m) high – completely impassable for any distance. There are gigantic areas of wilderness, and then you come upon open lagoons amidst the reed-beds. The Russians call them 'ilmens' and they gradually grow larger, as the reeds are confined to small islands, and finally run out into open water.

CHAPTER SEVEN

THE FIERY PENINSULA

There is no other peninsula in the world quite like it. Twenty-nine (some say 33) active volcanoes, including the 15,580ft (4750 m) Klyuchevskaya Sopka, one of the highest and most active volcanoes in the world. Titanic eruptions of red-hot lava and volcanic ash. Earthquakes and tidal waves. A steaming valley of geysers shooting boiling water 130 ft (40 m) into the air. Unique fir trees, traditionally sacred to the local people. Gigantic plants. Rivers teeming with spawning salmon. The largest bear in the Soviet Union, weighing up to 1500 lb (700 kg). An eagle with a 10-ft (3 m) wing-span. Kamchatka has them all.

This remote, spear-shaped peninsula 4000 miles (6500 km) from Moscow projects southwards into the northern Pacific between the Bering Sea and the Sea of Okhotsk. It has been described recently by Anatoly Filatov, writing in *Soviet Weekly*, as an 'extraordinary terrain, the bowels of the Earth ripped open by nature . . . a shrine for geologists, vulcanologists and botanists, where one can watch rock formation processes that elsewhere were completed millions of years ago'.

Kamchatka is twice the size of Britain with less than a hundredth of its population (460,000). Its wildlife, vegetation and landscape are all shaped by intense volcanic activity. Klyuchevskaya Sopka, for instance, continues to emit the steam and smoke it has been producing for over 8000 years — between eruptions — and as recently as 1975 one valley (Tolbachik) gave birth to four new volcanoes. New ones are still being added to the list.

It is Kamchatka's position in the 'Pacific Fiery Ring' which makes it so volcanically active. This gigantic ring runs around the rim of the Pacific

An apparently dormant volcano in the Kamchatka range.

Ocean in a colossal northward sweep from New Zealand and then south almost to the very tip of South America. Kamchatka lies within this ring between Japan and the Kuril Islands to the south and the Aleutian Islands to the east. It is all a question of plate tectonics, of the huge, slow-moving plates which make up the earth's crust and slide, converge and separate. Offshore a deep ocean trench is created where the Pacific Ocean plate slides downwards to be consumed in the earth's hot interior. Inland this continuous and inexorably slow movement produces fracturing of the earth's crust accompanied by earthquakes. As Kamchatka lies at the meeting place of not just two but three tectonic plates, it is especially active.

Not unnaturally, the peninsula is the home of the USSR Academy of Sciences' Institute of Vulcanology. Its scientists observe eruptions from dangerous proximities, parachute onto smoking summits and monitor underground activity with instruments linked to a communications satellite which allows them to process information fast. With the volcanoes as their laboratory, they are also dramatically investigating the genesis of life. They have discovered amino and nucleic acids – components of a living cell – in volcanic ash, giving rise to speculation that life could have begun in the depths of the earth's inferno. The warm sides of the volcano incubate these basic life-forms, prompting one Soviet vulcanologist to refer to volcanoes as 'caring nannies'.

Kamchatka's landscape is being constantly formed by its volcanoes. Some emit fumes constantly, some only occasionally. Pulverised lava shoots sporadically from the gaping crater mouths and flaming incandescent gas can be seen at night for miles. Kamchatka has been rocked by the full force of volcanic eruptions many times this century, but none on the scale of Bezymyanny in 1956. Imagine several hundred large earth tremors lasting for several weeks, then a huge explosion equivalent to a 7-megaton atomic bomb, followed by a thick cloud of black ash cut through by forked lightning, accompanied by ash and mud flows, formed from the melted snow, tearing down the mountainsides.

Ash and lava flow may destroy relentlessly but there is compensation in their rich mineral content and the consequent fertility which may take thousands of years to build up. Even more destructive can be the effects of volcanic eruptions or earthquakes on the seabed off the coast. *Tsunamis* or seismic sea waves (also sometimes called tidal waves) race towards the land at heights of up to 100 ft (30 m) and destroy everything before them.

But in the long term the volcanoes have a more serious effect on the natural world. In the Kronotsky nature reserve's Valley of Geysers, for instance, other kinds of volcanic activity (not just ash and lava flow) can be lethal. The bodies of dead bears, birds and other creatures have been found at the foot of the Kikhpinich volcano, poisoned by the high local concentration of hydrogen sulphide, and there has been a particularly severe death toll among the birds, crows included, which feed off the poisoned corpses.

This phenomenon is not confined to Kamchatka. The well-known naturalist Bernhard Grzimek wrote in the 1960s about the active volcanoes in East Africa's Kivu Park, where carbon dioxide can reach a 40-percent concentration on windless nights and kill much wildlife, paralysing it first

so that birds and bats, for instance, plummet to the ground. In one place 25 dead elephants were found, in another a great many baboons as well as lions, antelope, rhinoceroses, reptiles and other animals. Hyenas and griffons drawn by the carcasses themselves perished, adding to the mountains of corpses and bones.

Steam and lava erupt from one of the 29 active volcanoes of the Kamchatka peninsula.

However, some effects of volcanoes are beneficial. In an age where harnessing natural energy has become a vital alternative to the traditional nuclear, oil and coal industries, exploiting the heat which volcanoes bring to the earth's surface is one viable option. Tapping high-pressure sources of natural steam, an 11-megawatt geothermal power station has been serving the inhabitants of Kamchatka since 1967.

Flora and fauna also benefit from the peninsula's volcanoes and numerous geysers. Blue and green algae thrive in the warm, naturally-heated springs, turning the water olive-green, and in these natural 'hot-houses' imported species of fish, such as sturgeon, are now being bred.

A classic example of the volcanoes' beneficence to nature lies in the 42 square-mile (108 sq km) caldera, or enormous basin-shaped crater caused by collapse, of 5300-ft (1617 m) Mount Uzon, where vulcanologists and geologists can observe mineralization taking place, a process that normally takes millions of years. The caldera is dotted with hot springs, small mud volcanoes, an abundance of fumaroles (vents through which vapours and hot gases escape) and hundreds of large muddy ponds bubbling from the fumaroles beneath them.

Musk oxen were reintroduced to Russia from North America. The bulls' distinctive horns are adapted to competition by head-butting.

All this heat keeps the ponds and swamps at up to 194 °F (90 °C) and prevents some of them freezing over in the intensely cold winter; and the temperature and fertile ash combine to produce lush vegetation when outside the caldera all is bleak upland tundra. Here, for instance, are groves of dwarf stone birch (*Betula lanata*), Siberian pine and rowan, and the high grass projects even above the deep snow in winter. Virtually defying the seasons, Uzon's astonishing caldera attracts tens of thousands of waterfowl each year, among them geese, swans and ducks, such as teal and merganser. Some of them, swans included, have little reason to migrate each year to the warmer south and winter in this climatic oasis instead.

Reindeer and musk ox, bear and sable, marmot and ermine all make their way to this haven where there are no winter blizzards to present them with food problems and buds appear prematurely. Fledglings, fed on the mineral-rich offerings of the crater, grow at an unusually fast pace. Is this, perhaps, Russia's Garden of Eden?

The two native peoples of this extraordinary peninsula, the 1500-odd Itelmen and 7600-odd Koryaks, are now greatly outnumbered by Russians, and the Itelmen, Kamchatka's original population, are now much inter-married. In the eighteenth century they were still in the Stone Age. Today they usually live along rivers in fishing collectives, hunt fur-bearing animals and, more than any other northern Siberian people, gather wild plants and their products including berries, sweet grass stems, arnica leaves, pine nuts and above all the edible bulbs of the black fritillary (*Fritillaria kamtschatica*). Traditionally they mixed their tobacco with birch fungus ash and wove nettle fibre into fishing nets.

Like so many other fishing peoples of northern Asia, the Itelmen turned most of their catch into *yukola*, gutted fish dried in the sun and wind on special racks, allowing some, however, to ferment in pits before consumption. Fish eyes were a delicacy. Each house had hooks for hanging fish and, according to one Itelmen writer, Natalya Selivanova, 'Everything in the house smelled of fish, and there were dogs and puppies everywhere.' Bears, she relates, were regarded with superstition but the Itelmen, nonetheless, traditionally applied bear fat to wounds. Intriguingly, the bears rub their own wounds against 'bear's root' grass.

The Koryaks, related to the Itelmen linguistically, have, like some of the other numerically small peoples of the USSR, their own (officially) autonomous district of 116,000 square miles (300,000 sq km) which, particularly after the August revolution of 1991, may eventually see true autonomy. Most of them are reindeer herders and breeders living inland, and traditionally nomadic according to the needs of their reindeer. In winter they move from one pasture to another when grazing is exhausted. Spring brings the hard work of protecting pregnant does from predators. In summer they drive the herds to mountain pastures near rivers full of fish and in autumn bring them back to the family camp.

As with the other reindeer peoples, the Koryaks' reindeer provided them with almost all their material needs: skins for shirts, trousers, mittens and one-piece garments for babies and small children; skins also, waterproofed by smoking, for tents; tendons for thread. Reindeer meat, boiled, was the main diet, together with the raw marrow, tendons, gristle and kidney.

These reindeer Koryaks joined the fishing Koryaks on the coast when Kamchatka's incredible numbers of fish began to spawn. The coastal Koryaks were not only fishermen but hunted seals from their sealskin kayaks, used sealskin for straps and boot soles, and ate seal meat and blubber, using the latter for tallow as well. They also hunted sable, wolverine, bears and wild reindeer, but always tried to avoid killing wolves, believing them to be kinsmen.

Like the Itelmen, the Koryaks gathered plants: grass for lining boots and weaving baskets and mats; fly-agaric (*Amanita muscaria*), the hallucinogenic mushroom, to induce trances in the shaman; crowberry and blueberry to be eaten raw or mixed with grated reindeer or seal meat, fat and edible roots; sedge, wild sorrel and willow-herb as seasoning. The *yukola*, their main food through the year, was stored in reindeer tents on high piles under dried grass, and fed the dogs as well.

Koryak ritual and mythology were closely bound to the natural world. The master of the earth was Kujkynnjaku, the Raven, who also served as protector for the tribes. Dogs were sacrificed to ensure good hunting and their bodies impaled on tall stakes with their muzzles pointing to the east. Reindeer bones and antlers were placed in sacred sites to venerate the ancestral spirit, and bears which had been shot were greatly honoured, the skull's orifices bedecked with pine branches as part of an elaborate ritual.

An aerial view of the snow-clad peaks of Kamchatka's mountain ranges.

The old Koryak beliefs and customs may be disappearing under contemporary pressure, and some Koryaks are now teachers, doctors, engineers, vets and so on, but the lives of most are still closely bound to nature. Traditionally, they feared punishment by the spirits if they killed more animals than were essential to their existence – a good principle for Western societies to adopt.

Certainly the multitudes of Pacific salmon spawning each year in Kamchatka's waters must have given the indigenous peoples cause to bless nature. One reason for the abundance of salmon is, once again, the peninsula's volcanoes. The rich mineral content of volcanic ash in the rivers helps create an ideal spawning ground for the prolific fish. After Bezymyanny's tremendous eruption in 1956, a great deal of ash fell into many lakes which now contain larger populations of salmon than those which escaped the ash. Fisheries are now using pools warmed by thermal springs to produce salmon which gain weight four times faster than they would normally.

Kamchatka's waterways are the birthplace of huge populations of Pacific salmon, among them the keta or chum (*Oncorhynchus keta*), the sockeye (*O. nerka*) and the gorbuscha or hump-backed salmon (*O. gorbuscha*). The latter's gaunt shape is acquired as it drags its 15-lb (7 kg) body upstream to spawn. The peninsula's salmon shoals are counted in millions when they return to spawn, the sockeye alone never leaving for the ocean but remaining in Kamchatka's lakes and rivers.

The life cycle of the salmon is one of nature's many wonders. In the clear rivers and streams of this remote peninsula the tiny fry develop from eggs to begin their long journey to the mid-Pacific, their home for the next year or two, and then return to the precise location where they were spawned to spawn themselves. It is during this vulnerable home run that the predators gather – bear, sable, fox, raven and man – to fish in the thrashing waters. After spawning the salmon die, their golden-red bodies turning an ashen silver. Even when dead they help to enrich nature's cycle, for their innumerable corpses fertilize the water and ensure better survival prospects for their descendants.

The salmon now accounts for most of the 1.5 million tons of fish caught on Kamchatka every year, representing a substantial income to the fishing industry. Unfortunately, however, like so many Soviet industries at present, fisheries are badly managed and there is a low standard of equipment both on boats and in canning factories. Furthermore, there is the almost standard lack of cooperation between the various authorities.

On a more positive note, experiments have recently shown that by adding phosphates to lakes it is possible to increase their productivity and significantly improve the young salmon's chances of survival and thus their overall population. The potential economic benefits of this have been conservatively put at 8–12 million roubles a year, although one may question the ecological consequences. A few years ago the USSR Ministry of Fisheries set up a programme to examine the biological, genetic and spawning patterns of the salmon, but to date it has made little impact on the environmental problems which threaten them. Biologists on Kamchatka are concerned by the increasing number of tourists and the expansion of

The white-tailed eagle shares the same habitat as the larger Steller's sea eagle. Both feed on migrating and spawning fish, especially salmon.

fishing, timber-felling, hunting and energy, and want proper control exercised over such enterprises in order to prevent environmental disaster.

As one geneticist, Valentin Kripichnikov, warned in *Priroda*, the USSR's excellent scientific magazine, 'Kamchatka must be protected, its natural riches preserved, and first in line must be the salmon.' For as in the case of the sable and the saiga, apparently limitless numbers can drop to near-extinction. Lake Kurilsk in the far south of Kamchatka was, and fortunately is once more, the largest spawning ground in the whole of Asia for the sockeye salmon. Yet, only fifteen years ago, the fish was under real threat of extinction here. Evgeny Lobkov, a local biologist, has explained what happened. Commercial fishing in the lake is intensive, and more than half its fish are caught annually. It was even higher in 1944, according to Lobkov, when Japan (not yet at war with the USSR) had concessional rights to the fish and caught up to 70 percent, and after the war higher still, at 77–89 percent between 1953 and 1975, when the Japanese fishing industry was using drifters. By the mid 1970s the sockeye population had plummeted to only 300–400,000 fish.

Urgent measures were required to save the Kurilsk salmon from extinction and in 1977 the USSR introduced a 200-mile (320 km) conservation zone and the following year imposed strict quotas, weight restrictions and a limited fishing season. Soviet fisheries began to comply, and the sockeye to increase. But as they did so, the food available for them started to decrease, and it was decided to fertilize the lake with phosphates.

This increased the food base for the young fish, so they entered the sea as stronger fish, more likely to survive. The population rose rapidly and in 1983 more than 1.5 million sockeye entered the lake to spawn. By 1987 the figure had doubled to 3 million, and by 1991 it had doubled again to more than 6 million, one reason being that the Japanese fishing boats received notification too late and missed the spawning season. (Lake Kurilsk is now, incidentally, affiliated to the Kronotsky nature reserve.)

Because of their huge numbers, explains Lobkov, sockeye spawn in the shallow water at the edge of the lake throughout the winter. This abundance of fish creates ideal conditions in which large raptors can winter, and in the last five years a unique ecosystem has developed. Directly dependent on the sockeye, there now winter here a great number of swans, ducks and other waterfowl as well as golden eagles, several dozen white-tailed eagles and, most dramatically of all, between 300 and 700 of one of the world's largest birds of prey, Steller's sea eagle (*Haliaeetus pelagicus*). This magnificent bird, with its huge yellow beak, the most powerful in the entire bird kingdom, was named after the brilliant eighteenth-century naturalist Georg-Wilhelm Steller, who sailed with Bering to discover Alaska and was later shipwrecked with him.

This great eagle's size is certainly impressive: the female (slightly larger than the male) measures 3 ft 3 in (1.02 m) from beak to tail with an 8–ft (2.5 m) wing-span. It is strikingly coloured, the predominantly brown plumage of the first year transformed in adulthood into an ochre-brown head, white throat, white tail with cinnamon-brown undertail, blackish-brown wings with large white patches and white 'trousers'. Remarkably, bones matching those of this huge bird have been found in Essex, evidence of its enormous original range.

Many of these eagles migrate from Kamchatka and the Bering Sea coast to Hokkaido, the northernmost island of Japan, where the bird is both a protected bird and a 'national monument'. A joint Soviet–Japanese survey in the winter of 1985–6 established a world population of over 6000, around 4000 of them in the USSR, just over 2000 in Japan and others widely scattered.

They return again to breed in the summer, Kamchatka's tree-lined valleys and salmon-filled rivers making an ideal nesting ground. The eyries, made of large branches, and sometimes 8 ft (2.5 m) in diameter, are normally built high in the tops of poplar, birch or larch trees but some sea eagles build nests on crags. One pair of Steller's sea eagles will often use the same nest for 4–6 years, repairing it if the harsh Kamchatka winds damage it. In March mating begins and the air is filled with hoarse screams. The female lays her clutch of 1–3 light-green eggs towards the end of April, and the chicks hatch in early June.

Although salmon are plentiful in Kamchatka at this time, it is common to see the sea eagles fight over fish, and Lobkov has found that 'They show all their beauty and skill in catching fish and in their disputes over the sockeye salmon, even though there are enough for them all and the fish are no trouble to catch, but they are probably too lazy to get into cold water . . .' The instigator of such fights, he notes, is usually one of the young birds which snatches fish from adults or one of its peer group.

By the end of July and beginning of August, the young eagles, reared on their salmon-rich diet, have grown to almost two-thirds their parents' size. By the end of August and occasionally as late as September they are ready for flight.

The recent joint Soviet–Japanese survey of the bird's numbers estimated that 60 percent winter on Kamchatka and the other 40 percent migrate to Japan's Shiretoko peninsula. Figures have shown a healthy increase of its world population from approximately 3000 to over 6000 since the early 1980s. Ironically, the inhabitants of Shiretoko attribute this to the Japanese fishing fleets' increased ability to fish in icy conditions so that fish which spill from their nets are now available to the sea eagle all the year round.

Sockeye salmon make up the main part of the sea eagle's diet and the abundance of dead salmon in any one place determines their wintering places. Other prey includes birds and mammals such as hare, young seal, Arctic fox and sable. They have also been reported feeding on marine refuse and carrion such as poisoned foxes and rotten fish, this perhaps *in extremis* for in particularly harsh winters they can die from lack of food.

Climatic changes are now having an effect on the sea eagles' behaviour. They use ice as a platform to lead them from one place to another, so that if the wind shifts the ice in the Sea of Okhotsk they move with it to roost on the nearest land. Since the winter of 1988–9, however, an increase in the sea's temperature has correspondingly decreased sea ice to a 'record minimum' and with it the sea eagle's movements, so that their numbers in any one place have remained more constant. However, it is too early to judge the effects of this change.

Many other species, not just the sea eagle, have Kamchatka's volcanic ash to thank, in part at least, for the teeming salmon. Among them is the bear and it may well be the abundance of these fish which explains both the size of the bears and their numbers. Kamchatka's bears are the biggest in the Soviet Union and weigh up to 1500 lb (700 kg) and are the world's largest bears after those of Alaska's Kodiak Island across the Bering Sea.

Until the eighteenth century bears inhabited Russia's wooded steppe as well as forests and, as land became cultivated and forests felled, the bear retreated even further. After the Second World War its numbers fell considerably in the western regions, and 'bear country' now lies predominantly in the east, with the greatest concentration of all on Kamchatka, which is sometimes known as 'bear corner'. A decade ago the estimate was 10,000, and now, in good years, there are up to 580 in the Kronotsky reserve alone.

Unlike other bears of the USSR, which tend to feed on one basic foodstuff at a time depending on the season, the Kamchatkan bear has a mixed diet, consuming in one day fish, berries and plants. It also digs out field voles, gophers and other rodents. In July when the hump-backed salmon returns to the rivers to spawn, many bears make their way from the mountains for the big catch, although about 20 percent remain on the slopes to hunt sockeye and goltsi salmon. In August and September bears near the coast add berries to their diet and in October consume Siberian pine nuts.

Nevertheless times can be bad and fish only seasonal. When, for instance, in 1968 and 1977 freak June temperatures dropped as far as 5 °F (−15 °C), producing only a scanty crop of berries and pine nuts, the resulting famine

Steller's sea eagle, one of the largest birds of prey in the world. The nest and young are perched in a precarious position, high on a cliff edge.

Male sockeye salmon in their spawning ground.

among the bears was so bad that some resorted to cannibalism. The females were even reported to have torn at their own flesh. Such a famine can reduce the bears of one region by 70–80 percent.

Kamchatka's bears make paths through the peninsula's dense vegetation, including 'tunnels' through the high grass of the rivers' flood meadows at spawning time. Indeed most of the few roads on Kamchatka were originally bear paths.

Russia's bear symbol may have been 'Disneyfied', particularly as Misha, the cuddly cartoon figure of Moscow's 1980 Olympics, but although Kamchatka's bears are generally less aggressive than in certain other parts of the country, man must always be on guard. Hunters have found themselves prey rather than predator. In 1975 the remains of one M. Potapov, hunter turned victim, were found next to his gun. Both had been dragged a third of a mile (0.5 km) from the place he had been killed, demonstrating the bear's strange habit of sitting on the belongings of its quarry. It also summons up an (albeit erroneous) image of a bear armed with a gun pursuing hunters!

More shy than threatening, Russia's brown bear – still particularly popular in Soviet circuses, unfortunately – may face a dangerous future as the Soviet authorities try to boost their foreign-currency earnings with expensive hunting trips. Already hunting lodges are springing up in northern Russia and across Siberia and visitors can shoot a bear and have it skinned and stuffed for $5000. How soon will this lucrative trade invade the bear haven of Kamchatka?

Just as Kamchatka is the home of the Soviet Union's largest bear, so too is its sable larger (and browner) than all others. It also has the most luxuriant fur of them all, and so is greatly sought after. In the eighteenth century William Tooke, a member of Russia's Imperial Academy of Sciences wrote that at the time of the Russian conquest of Kamchatka:

> the sables were there in such extraordinary numbers, that a single hunter could easily bring away sixty, eighty, and more of these animals in the winter, and they were held in such little estimation by the Kamchatdels that they deemed the more useful skin of a dog to be of twice the value. For ten roubles worth of iron-ware there was no difficulty in obtaining the value of five or six hundred roubles in sables; and whoever had only followed this trade to Kamchatka for the space of a year, usually came back with a profit of thirty thousand roubles and upwards.

Indeed for hundreds of years the Kamchatka sable has been the peninsula's chief export. Its hunting intensified in the mid nineteenth century, when both demand and price increased. In 1841, for instance, Kamchatka exported nearly 10,000 sable pelts and the rate increased, so that towards the end of the century the population had dropped so sharply that there was a real threat of extinction.

In 1882, therefore, Benedict Dybowski, an enlightened Polish doctor, zoologist and former Siberian exile, set up with local support a wildlife reserve where sable hunting was banned and where guards patrolled in winter, the hunting season. This protection lasted until the early years of this century. In 1934 almost exactly the same area became the Kronotsky Nature Reserve of 3860 square miles (10,990 sq km) but now with the aim of protecting not only the sable but the area's entire wildlife. But despite measures by the government to protect the sable here and at Barguzin, poaching continued even in the new reserves. Nevertheless by the end of the 1940s the sable's temporary reprieve had allowed it to increase its numbers and spread across the peninsula. In the decade 1959–69 a maximum of 10,200 sables were caught annually on Kamchatka.

Nowadays some 70 percent of Kamchatka's sables inhabit the peninsula's 21,600 square miles (56,000 sq km) of stone birch forests which cover mountain slopes and are distinguishable by the closeness of the treetops and the thick, grassy undergrowth beneath. Field voles and other small rodents, a major part of the sable's diet, thrive in these conditions, and hollow trees and fallen twigs create ideal nesting conditions for the sable itself. Groves of mountain ash usually provide abundant berries, but in severe winters with food shortages the sable is forced to move down to the valleys, even though, being strongly territorial, it leaves its established hunting areas only with reluctance. In winter its weight drops 4 oz (100 gm) from an average 3¼ lb (1460 gm) in January (adult male) to 3 lb (1360 gm) in March.

Unlike other sables, the sable of Kamchatka includes fish in its diet (despite its preference for berries), and the availability of fish gives it a better chance of survival in a poor berry year, as is the case with the Kamchatkan brown bear. Even so, survival can be tough. V. N. Shnitnikov, a biologist of the Kronotsky reserve, has described the desperation of sable during one particularly harsh winter:

> There had been a catastrophic harvest one autumn and the main source of food for predators was scarce. Exceptionally deep winter blizzards prevented access to the food which lay beneath it. The sables began to starve and moved closer and closer to human habitation, foraging around the rubbish dumps like feral cats. In the centre of the reserve where the settlement stood sables ran in and out of houses, charged along the streets in broad daylight, climbed into the kitchen and canteen etc. Many of them learned to recognize the dinner bell and on hearing it shot out of the woods to the canteen. People were amazed at this display of trust and fearlessness from these beautiful animals and willingly threw them titbits of food.

The Kamchatka sable breeds from mid April to the end of May, slightly later than the sable of southern Siberia. Its relatively low birth rate plays an important role in regulating hunting numbers. The fertility of the female sable increases as she matures and her annual litter can begin with one and end with eight young. After six weeks in the nest the young leave and by August the family have split up.

Sables, bears, sea eagles, salmon and indeed the whole spectrum of Kamchatka's wildlife have a safe haven in the Kronotsky nature reserve on the peninsula's east coast, which has an area of 4240 square miles (10,990 sq km). Established in 1934 as a conservation area for endangered fauna, especially the Kamchatkan sable, it was made a biosphere reserve in 1984.

The Kronotsky reserve incorporates all the natural zones of Kamchatka and is home to more than 700 species of higher plants of tundra, taiga and mountain. This is relatively low compared to the 1600 or so higher plants of the Caucasus reserve, for instance, owing to Kamchatka's special climate, vulcanism and isolation. And yet there is much of interest here, including endemic plants such as the Kamchatka dropwort (*Filipendula kamtschatica*) and Kamchatka goat's beard (*Aruncus kamtschatica*), and in Kronotsky's mild climate and fertile soil plants grow to extraordinary sizes, particularly the dropwort, which in its brief vegetation cycle can grow up to 4 in (10 cm) in 24 hours to form 13–ft (4 m) high thickets.

Willow and maple line the reserve's river banks, Siberian pine and alder grow on hill slopes and the stone birch (*Betula ermani*) – sometimes 600 years old – forms sparse upland forests. But the most unusual tree is the endemic Kamchatka fir (*Abies gracilis*), relict of the pre-ice age coniferous forests, which survives only in one small part of Kronotsky and nowhere else in the world.

The reserve's director, V. Vavinov, enthuses about the natural treasures of his domain, including one of its less obvious features, beloved (and enjoyed) across the country by countless generations of Russians:

> Mushrooms grow not only in the forest but also on the tundra. Sometimes you look and can hardly believe what you see: is this a dream or is it real? Standing out above the tundra are the huge hats of the orange-cap and brown-cap boletus together with the edible white mushroom. Where else can you see such a sight?

The sea otter is an extremely agile animal; it can float on its back while using 'tools' such as stones to extract food from within hard shells or cases.

The reserve's most famous feature, however, is the Valley of Geysers, remarkably only discovered in 1941. Here, in an 8-mile (5 km) stretch, 22 large and active geysers erupt every three or four seconds, the most powerful of them, 'Vulcan', ejecting a jet of boiling water 130 ft (40 m) high with the steam reaching 1000 ft (300 m). Here, too, are bubbling mud pools, boiling multi-coloured lakes, and pulsating springs. To paraphrase one Russian description, the whole valley steams, rumbles, gurgles, splashes and snorts. And its comparatively high temperature and humidity bring early spring and lush emerald-green vegetation, including giant herbaceous plants such as dropwort and bedstraw.

Kronotsky's five active volcanoes (there are also 11 extinct ones) emit gas and vapour when not erupting. On the one hand the ash from their eruptions supplies nutrients for plants and thus benefits the animal world too; on the other hand eruptions can cover large areas with hot ash, often wiping out all vegetation and very many animals.

Kronotskaya Sopka, the reserve's highest and splendidly symmetrical volcano at 11,575 ft (3528 m) is Kamchatka's second highest after Klyuchevskaya Sopka and its full height rises majestically from its surroundings, its snow-capped peak visible 125 miles (200 km) away. On its slopes and those of the reserve's other volcanoes lie 19 square miles (50 sq km) of glaciers, blackened by volcanic ash and dust.

In 1985, 580 square miles (1500 sq km) of coastal waters were added along Kronotsky's 125-mile (200 km) coastline, where many birds and mammals congregate. The steep rocks are the home in summer for vociferous colonies of gulls and auks such as guillemots and tufted puffins (*Lunda cirrhata*), cormorants, and sea eagles, predating on the many varieties of fish in the sea and river mouths. Sandy beaches are imprinted with the paws of many animals including the brown bear, which makes its way to the numerous waterfalls flowing into the sea, enticed by teeming shoals of spawning salmon. Foxes, hares and deer also find food and mineral salt along this rich coastline.

Kronotsky's remotest rocks provide the largest breeding ground of the Northern or Steller's sea lion (*Eumetopias jubata*) which arrives each spring after wintering in the warmer Sea of Japan and departs again in October. Here too are ringed seals (*Phoca hispida*), common seals (*P. vitulina*) and the sea otter (*Enhydra lutris*), once almost exterminated for its thick and extremely valuable fur. A ban on its hunting east of Kamchatka in the Commander Islands (one of its original homes) was imposed in 1912, followed by another ban in 1926 after the Revolution, but it is listed as rare in the Red Book of the USSR, although happily sea otters are appearing more and more often along the Kronotsky reserve coast and both their population and distribution area are gradually increasing. Known as Kamchatka beavers for their superb dexterity in the water, these appealing creatures consume fish, crabs, molluscs and sea urchins while lying on their backs on the sea's surface.

The Kronotsky reserve is also particularly rich in bird life. One Soviet ornithologist noted 128 species during his investigations between 1940 and 1946. Now there are 212 species, presumably because hitherto unrepresented birds have sought refuge here. Besides the sea birds there are the many cuckoos, woodpeckers and nightingales of the birch groves, the ducks, geese and other waterfowl of the lakes and rivers, and the buff-breasted pipit (*Anthus nibescens*) and snow buntings (*Plectrophenax nivalis*) of the volcanic slopes.

The reserve's animals are far fewer: only 37 species, including sable, ermine, wolf, bear, 3000 herds of wild reindeer, and the rare bighorn sheep (*Ovis canadensis*), which migrates in spring down from the highlands to the coast for food and badly needed salt.

No wonder that this area, so incredibly rich in wildlife and volcanic activity, is a biosphere reserve too, and recognized as of international importance. It is also very possible that in the near future it may become, very properly, a World Heritage Site. Given its isolated position and remarkable range of natural treasures, we can only hope that it will forever escape the environmental problems threatening so many other parts of the country and indeed the globe. Like many other Soviet nature reserves, it will perhaps become a kind of twenty-first-century Noah's Ark.

Unique this remarkable peninsula may be in so many respects, yet there is one part of this vast country still unexamined and in its own way even more surprising to find, considering the traditional image of the Soviet Union. It lies in the extreme south-east, south-west of Kamchatka across the Sea of Okhotsk: a totally different world from the rest of the Soviet Union in climate, flora and fauna. It is a huge northern monsoon forest with climbing vines and lianas, cork trees, ginseng and a mass of medicinal plants. Here are exotic birds and butterflies, poisonous snakes, rare leopards and, not least, the largest member of the cat family, the magnificent Siberian tiger.

Arvidas Baronas, cameraman on Kamchatka

We filmed the sea eagles in winter. In general there were fewer than usual but further from the lake more sea eagles remained in the same breeding site. We saw the young Steller's sea eagle very close to our hide, not yet with the white adult shoulder plumage. When we awoke in the mornings there would always be eagles around.

We often passed the den of a fox which sometimes accompanied us to the door of our hide. It did not normally appear during the day when it was nagged by crows.

We moved into another hide nearer to the Steller's sea eagles. One even landed on the roof of the hide when we were cooking lunch, then swooped off to catch a fish. Normally the eagles slowly fly down to a stream, catch fish in their talons and pull them ashore. They sit in trees or on the shore without doing anything for such a long time that it is impossible to guess when they will hunt. The eagles seem to enjoy conflicts; it is usually the young birds which try to take away another's catch. Old birds seem more peaceable, especially when dealing with the younger birds.

On one occasion we set up camp in a geyser valley, and spent a day rushing from one geyser to another. Sometimes the geysers emptied every four to six hours; sometimes they filled the whole valley with steam, making it difficult to see, and splashing us with small drops of water half a kilometre (550 yards) away. Judging by the smell the water could well have been acidic.

We went to explore the waterfalls and geysers at Sakhany, Sosed and Troinoy. It was not easy going. At times we had to walk on top of the knife-edged mountain ridge or in the middle of a steep slope. There is a great array of colourful natural clays but after it had rained the soles of our shoes immediately became covered in clay, cushioning our steps. Below us lay the Geizerny River and boiling mud and water.

We discovered a small geyser close to the river which acted as a successful equivalent to the modern washing machine. After 20 minutes, the geyser would disappear into the bowels of the earth leaving the clean and boiled washing on the stones of its crater.

We moved on to Bormotino where we found an occupied sea eagle's nest with a downy chick inside. The pair of adult eagles became used to our presence after a couple of days and were surprisingly silent in contrast to other types of bird which announce their arrival with several short cries. The eagles did everything in complete silence and so we found it difficult to detect their arrival at the nest. When we began filming, the female adult was still feeding the chick but later the parent birds would merely throw fish into the nest to allow the chick to feed itself.

In addition we were able to settle close to the nest of an Aleutian tern, a beautiful bird listed in the Red Data Book. It was incubating its eggs and would tidy the nest and produce sounds similar to the purring of a cat, distinct from the harsh cries of the other terns and gulls.

CHAPTER EIGHT

NORTH MEETS SOUTH

Few in the West have much conception of the easternmost regions of the Soviet Union bordering the Pacific Ocean – apart from the fact that on the coastline lies Vladivostok, the terminus of the 5000-mile (8047 km) long Trans-Siberian railway. Certainly the people living there in the same longitudes as Australia and New Zealand regard it not as Siberia but as the Soviet Far East, while in Tsarist days it was the Russian Far East, a name to which it may well soon return.

Its extreme south-eastern region, on the Sea of Japan, is an outstandingly interesting area and without question very different indeed from the tundra and taiga of the rest of northern Asia. Here, between the mouth of the Amur and the borders of China and North Korea, mostly along the River Amur and its tributary, the Ussuri, the taiga which has stretched for so many thousands of miles merges into a northern monsoon forest with a remarkable range of exotic and endemic flora and fauna found nowhere else in the USSR. It is here that is found the most remarkable nature of all Russia, very far indeed from the popular image of the country.

Whereas much of the USSR suffers from a markedly continental climate, with extremes of temperature – hot summers and icy winters – and generally low rainfall, this far eastern location gives it a unique and quite different climate: in summer the south-eastern monsoon winds bring moist tropical air and rain is plentiful, sometimes falling in almost tropical deluges, of up to 10 in (25 cm) in one day.

But it is far from being tropical. The moderating Pacific ocean air staves off the snow until October in the Sikhote Alin mountains inland and later

Fungus growing on a dead tree within the forest covering the Sikhote Alin mountain-sides.

still along the coast, but when winter has arrived it is dominated by the freezing air flowing from the heart of the continent, bringing biting cold, clear skies and occasional light snowfall (heaviest late in the winter). At this time of year the *gornyaki* (north-western winds, literally 'mountain winds') rip along the coastal areas at more than 60 mph (100 kmph), tearing at the trees and whipping up the thin snow, laying bare the mountain tops. As if in a battle between the bulk of Asia and the vast Pacific, the icy Siberian air keeps the land in the grip of winter until as late as May, and spring is beset with frosts before the ocean air can once again warm the land.

Russia gained this area only in the last century, annexing from a weakened China territory north of the Amur in 1858 and east of the Ussuri in 1860. It meant a further extension of empire, strategic waterways and the foundation of a naval port on the Pacific, Vladivostok (meaning 'Hold the East!'). The town was built with much Chinese labour, but the Chinese have gone, expelled to their motherland by Stalin. Until shortly before the Second World War it was still regarded as pioneer country, a kind of 'wild east'. Today, other than Vladivostok and Khabarovsk, near the confluence of the Amur and Ussuri, it is still thinly populated, linked to the rest of the USSR by air, the Trans-Siberian track and new BAM railways.

In common with the other small peoples of the Soviet Union, the native peoples of the area, such as the 2,500 Ulchi and 10,000 Nanai (1979 figures), have had little say in the fate of their land. They have lived in harmony with nature, taking only what they themselves needed or required for trade, and traditionally they have held nature in high esteem.

The Pacific salmon spawns along the tributaries of the Amur as well as on the Kamchatka peninsula, and several of the indigenous peoples, including the Nanai (or Goldi as they were called before the Revolution), used to wear costumes of fishskin: light, durable and waterproof and not at all 'fishy' as one might imagine but cured, white in colour and, for festive occasions, beautifully decorated with geometric designs of Chinese influence.

These peoples, as well as many of the other Siberian races, may well be distantly related to the North American Indians, having common ancestors, some of whom remained in Asia while others crossed Beringia (the Bering land-bridge) into a new continent in prehistoric times. Even earlier, Beringia, like Eurasia and North America, was covered with a colossal deciduous forest containing, for instance, maples, walnuts, oaks and limes. Climatic changes millions of years ago moved the forest south into three separate areas: south-eastern Europe, eastern North America and the Ussuri region. All three areas today still contain many of the same families of trees, with fairly small differences between the species, considering the enormous time-scale over which these differences have evolved.

The Ussuri region's enormous variety of plants and animals is therefore, in part anyway, due to its history as part of this once gigantic forest, but it is also due to its position: south of the vast taiga, north of the forests of South-East Asia and east of the Himalayas. Forest species have moved into the area from north and south and mountain species from west; and the 700-mile (1130 km) Sikhote Alin mountain chain, parallel with the coastline and rising to nearly 6000 ft (1830 m), provides a wealth of habitats, suitable for many different plants and animals.

A woodman on horseback in the Sikhote Alin Reserve.

Here therefore are to be found representatives of all three regions, such as the elk, wolf, brown bear and sable of the Siberian taiga, the Himalayan or Asian black bear (*Selenarctos thibetanus*), its range stretching from Iran to Japan, the mountain-dwelling goral (*Naemorhaedus goral*) of the Himalayas, and the leopard (*Panthera pardus*) and dhole (*Cuon alpinus*) of South-East Asia. Animals and plants being no respecters of national frontiers, the mixed forest extends west into north-east China and south into Korea.

Many of the animals are distinct subspecies endemic to the region, the most famous being the Siberian tiger (*Panthera tigris altaica*), also known as the Manchurian, Amur or Ussuri tiger; others include the Ussuri black bear (*Selenarctos thibetanus ussuricus*), the Ussuri sika (*Cervus nippon hortulorum*) and the Amur leopard (*Panthera pardus orientalis*). Much of this unusual wildlife is rare, or even endangered as in the case of the leopard. Fortunately six nature reserves cover a considerable area. One of the biggest and most important is the Sikhote Alin Reserve (and Biosphere Reserve)

Thawing ice on Blagodatnoye Lake in the Sikhote Alin Reserve.

about 375 miles (600 km) north of Vladivostok, created in 1935 and embracing an area of 1342 square miles (3476 sq km).

It represents this whole ecosystem in microcosm, rising from the sea to a height of 5243 ft (1598 m) and is criss-crossed by rivers and mountain chains, with a scattering of lakes. Significantly, it contains flora and fauna representative of both northern and southern 'Ussuriland' with as many as 340 species of bird recorded within its boundaries.

The wealth and variety of the forest are immense. The bare, tundra-like mountain tops are surrounded by a green sea of a myriad of different trees, with tall Korean pines mingling with oaks, maples, walnuts and birches. Unlike the Siberian taiga, these forests have a well-developed undergrowth with abundant shrubs and low trees providing food and shelter for many of the birds and animals. Lianas and vines trail from trunks and branches, and the heady smells of honeysuckle and clematis sometimes fill the air.

Some of the trees are remarkable, and many of the birches of the region are quite different from the light-barked birches of Europe and North America and are regarded as more ancient 'primitive' species. They are darker-barked, slower-growing and longer-lived, one such species being called 'iron birch' (*Betula schmidtii*) in Russian because its wood is reputedly so heavy that it sinks in water.

One tree of vital importance to the forest is the Korean pine (*Pinus koraiensis*), which reaches heights of nearly 150 ft (46 m) and produces an enormous crop of cones, with each one yielding up to 200 nuts, rich in

nutritious oils. Most of the cones fall in autumn, but some fall throughout the year, providing a feast for the denizens of the forest floor, such as the wild boar (*Sus scrofa*), the brown bear (*Ursus arctos*), the Manchurian wapiti (*Cervus elaphus xanthopygas*) and even the sable (*Martes zibellina*). Many of the cones are raided while still attached to the tree by birds such as the nutcracker (*Nucifraga caryocatactes*) as well as squirrels and, perhaps surprisingly, the Ussurian black bear. A subspecies of the Asian black bear, it is smaller than its distant cousin the brown bear, generally weighing less than 400 lb (180 kg) and around 6 ft (2 m). All races of the Asian black bear have glossy black fur with a bright white V on their chest, while the Ussuri race can be distinguished by its longer, softer fur.

Surprising it may be to find a six foot mammal staring down from high up in the trees, but this is where the Ussuri black bear spends much of its time. It climbs easily, springing up any tree, gripping the trunk with its long, curved claws before finding a branch to perch on. This agility allows it to be largely vegetarian, enjoying a rich diet of fruit, berries and nuts such as those of the Korean pine. In other parts of Asia the different subspecies do not have access to such abundance of forage and in the Himalayas these bears are known as aggressive killers of livestock. Here, however, they are regarded much more benignly, with only occasional stories of people being attacked when disturbing a bear feasting on a rich supply of fruit. The Chinese, when they were here, used to call it the 'man-bear' because of its frequently upright posture and questioning gaze.

Lakes in the Sikhote Alin Reserve. Animals frequently come down to the shoreline to feed and hunt.

The black bear's life is intimately linked with the trees and it finds, if it can, a large hollow, well above the ground, in the rotten heart of a big, old tree for a winter den. Suitable trees may actually have several bears (and perhaps even other animals) on different levels, forming a bizarre apartment block. One or two cubs are born into this snug arboreal environment sometime in February, and three months or so later they venture out into the forest. At the first sign of danger their mother sends them scurrying up into the trees, a safe haven from the wolves although not, of course, man. This bear has been hunted for centuries both for its beautiful fur and for its gall bladder, which is still used by the Chinese as one of their many traditional medicines derived from animal products. The former Chinese of the region used a variety of hunting methods such as traps and pits to avoid direct contact with an enraged wounded animal. By far the most cunning was a honey-covered bomb which would kill any poor delighted bear anticipating a feast instead of its own immediate demise. Fortunately the black bear of the Ussuri forest is still quite common despite its relentless persecution and the reserves provide a welcome refuge for them.

The trees of the Ussuri forest yield abundant food for such hungry creatures and it is, perhaps, surprising that any of the nuts and seeds ever get a chance to grow and replace the trees that produce them. It is strange that trees such as Korean pine produce such palatable nuts, and we might expect evolution to have favoured those species with inedible or toxic seed to ensure adequate propagation. However, nature is rarely obvious and the tempting fruits and nutritious nuts give the trees and plants a perfect method for dispersal. Some pass undamaged through the gut of the wild boar, which effectively plants them ready fertilized, while disturbing the ground with its snout. Animals which prepare underground hoards, such as the squirrel and the nutcracker, sometimes forget a hiding place or two, allowing a patch of seedlings to sprout far from the parent plant.

In such ways many of the animals of this forest help maintain the rich mixture of tree species. However, if the density of these nut and fruit eaters becomes too high, most of the seed gets consumed and the forest's regeneration is severely hampered. Predators keep the numbers of such animals down as part of the forest's complex and dynamic equilibrium.

The complexity of these mixed forests of Ussuriland guarantees a vast range of food and habitats, reflected in the wealth of animal life, especially birds. The region's lakes are ideal for the wide variety of water birds such as the rare Japanese or Manchurian crane (*Grus japonensis*), now known to breed at only two sites, one on the island of Hokkaido and the other at Lake Khanka on the Soviet-Chinese border. This beautiful bird, with its all-white body, elegant black neck and elongated drooping black tertiary feathers, suffered dramatically during the Korean war, which reduced it to its present range. Now under threat of extinction, its population has fallen to only 249 (345 in 1983) in Japan, roughly 400 in north-east China and 200 in the USSR (1980) figures. Indeed many of them migrate through Korea, with others travelling to South-East Asia, Indonesia, Japan and even Australia. Recognizing the vulnerability of migratory birds, the USSR and Japan recently signed a comprehensive treaty intended to conserve their shared populations.

A Manchurian or Japanese crane engaged in a 'dance'. 'Dances' may be seen at any time of the year but are at their most intricate between a mated pair. Variations in individual movements alternate with jumps in the air.

Perhaps the most unusual bird to patrol the river systems east of the Amur and Ussuri (as well as further up the coastline and on Sakhalin Island) is Blakiston's fish owl (*Ketupa blakistoni*). There are two subspecies of this remarkable bird, one (*K. b. doerriesi*) occupying the continental part of the species' range from Magadan south along the Sea of Okhotsk coast to south Ussuriland and north-east China, the other (*K. b. blakistoni*) restricted to part of Hokkaido and Sakhalin Island and the south Kuril Islands. The fish owl was regarded as a deity by the native Ainu people because of its great size (some birds have a wing-span approaching 6½ ft [2 m]) and loud, haunting call, but unfortunately its numbers have dropped alarmingly due to deforestation to only 3–400 pairs in the USSR, so it, too, is under threat of extinction. The fish owl nests and hunts along wooded streams and rivers and, as such, the Russian population has a far greater range of suitable habitat than its Japanese cousin, for in the case of the latter the land has been largely cleared.

The owl usually hunts by perching in a branch overhanging the water and as soon as a fish strays too close, pounces, sometimes plunging deep into the water to grasp its prey in strong talons with which it crushes the life out of its victim. There are other fish owls elsewhere in the world, but this is by far the most northerly species and able to survive when the rivers and streams are frozen by hunting other prey on the ground or in the air. Although most skilled in the water, it will, when pressed, take hares and voles, and even snatch passing bats in deadly aerial combat. This flexibility allows it to

An azure-winged magpie feeding fledglings in the nest.

survive the bitter winter before it resumes fishing again in the spring. This impressive bird is strictly monogamous, and pairs bond together for 20 or so years, maintaining close contact when hunting, roosting and rearing chicks.

Another bird almost unique to the region is the azure-winged magpie (*Cyanopica cyana*). Smaller than its more ubiquitous cousin, the magpie (*Pica pica*), with its jet black head and wings and tail of a delicate powder blue, the most beautiful member of the crow family can be found throughout the Ussuri forests and also over 6000 miles (9600 km) away in the woods of Spain and Portugal. This bizarre distribution was at first thought to be due to the same changes in climate that caused the separation of the ancient mixed woodlands, but it is now believed that the bird was transported to Europe by early Portuguese or Spanish explorers hundreds of years ago.

Yet another outstanding feature of this mixed forest, so wealthy in the beauty and variety of its flora and fauna, is the concentration here of so many medicinal plants. The most famous of them is undoubtedly ginseng (*Panax ginseng*). Its plain green leaves on a stalk only about 2 ft (60 cm) high make it difficult to spot in the undergrowth – just as well, because it is disappearing after centuries of being dug up – but in late summer it can be easily identified by its crown of bright red berries. The root of this slow-growing plant, which can live for a hundred years, has been used from time immemorial as a miracle cure for general ill-health, an invigorating tonic and as an aphrodisiac. Its great rarity in the wild led to the powdered root at times being worth its weight in gold, and the much-revered plant, the subject of so much folklore was known as the 'root of life' by the local indigenous peoples, the Nanai and Udegey.

They believed that ginseng had a guardian, the largest animal of these forests, the Siberian tiger. It is easy to understand why it was worshipped and associated with great vigour and the vital forces of life. For this is the largest subspecies of tiger and the largest member of the cat family: up to nearly 12 ft (3.7 m) in length including a tail of around 3 ft (1 m), standing 4 ft (1.2 m) high at the shoulders and weighing about 550 lb (250 kg), with some exceptionally large males recorded at over 800 lb (360 kg). Larger, more powerful and more beautiful than the lion, this magnificent animal is surely the real 'King of the Beasts'. Indeed the Chinese character for 'King' closely resembles the mark on the Siberian tiger's forehead, but it is not known if this is due to coincidence or design.

The Siberian tiger is generally lighter in colour than other tigers, with large areas of white towards its chest and belly, and the predominantly yellow-orange or rich deep amber, the colour of dancing flames, interspersed with fine black stripes. In winter its fur lengthens and it is then that it looks especially splendid, a regal ruff around the male's massive throat.

This superlative creature is also found in Manchuria and the north of the Korean peninsula, but by far its largest concentration is in the Ussuri forest, where live 2–300 of the world's wild population (estimated at between 350 and 450 in 1990). Not only was it worshipped by the Nanai and Udegey, but it was also believed to possess near-magical powers by the erstwhile Chinese population who erected shrines to 'Lord Tiger' in the heart of the forest. Unfortunately this respect for the tiger's great power led to the use of almost all parts of the creature as rejuvenating medicines, believed to impart some of its strength to the consumer. Pure superstition perhaps, but it placed a very handsome price on every tiger when combined with the value of its splendid pelt. As the settlers in the Russian Far East increased around the turn of the century, the decline of the Siberian tiger was well under way. Large areas of lowland forest, especially near Lake Khanka, were cleared, widespread hunting of boars and deer greatly reduced the tiger's main prey, while the number of hunters grew, so around 150 tigers were killed every year. A combination of bad winters and diseases in the early part of this century further reduced the tiger's prey and by the 1940s there were only 20–30 left in the USSR, on the very brink of extinction. In 1948, therefore, the tiger was designated a protected animal in the USSR, and although some poaching continued, it recovered dramatically once it was protected and numbers climbed to their present level.

Like all tigers, the Siberian subspecies has quite complex and sophisticated behaviour, with a large home range, carefully patrolled and marked out, and a deadly hunting strategy. Since 1971, in the Sikhote Alin reserve, a dedicated team of Russian scientists has discovered much about its behaviour, spending the long winter months tracking tigers through the snow. Not only courage and perseverance but also considerable fitness are demanded for such a feat, as they have to cover many miles at a stretch with the temperature far below freezing. The occasional 'long drawn out wailing roar' they hear must fill them with a strange mixture of apprehension and gratification.

The tigers appear quite precise in their movements and often move in a virtually straight line for several miles, preferring to follow defined features such as the course of frozen rivers or the crest of a mountain ridge. These routes generally avoid unnecessary changes in altitude, as well as areas of deeper snow. In this way they usually cover 10–12 miles (16–19 km) a day, but can cover up to 60 miles (100 km) in a day when prey is in short supply. When they face a threat, they frequently backtrack as if choosing the line of quickest retreat. When they stay near prey for any length of time they pace out the tracks of their range in miniature, showing a detailed memory of their habitat and perhaps a little impatience.

Females have a territory of up to 150 square miles (390 sq km) and the male a territory sometimes two and a half times as big. Using its knowledge of the area, the tiger can move quickly along its system of paths to areas rich in prey or to its lair. It marks selected trees with urine and in places scrapes the ground to mark the boundaries of its domain. It has been suggested that this behaviour actually serves as a form of more complicated communication. Tigers are mostly solitary animals and a male's range overlaps another's only a little, but takes in a considerable part of a female's, who likewise avoids members of her own sex.

In January this solitude may be broken as the males and females come together to mate – quite a noisy affair – and the tigers stay together for some time in what is appropriately called a 'wedding', a time of play and cavorting about. After around 100 days two to four cubs are born and the solitary life of the tigress is suspended for a time. The cubs grow quickly and play a lot, frequently tumbling in the rivers and streams as they, like the adults, are great lovers of water: Siberian tigers have even been seen in rivers full of ice floes. The cubs may accompany their mother until they are nearly full grown and are sexually mature at three or four years of age. Remarkably, under ideal conditions the tiger's reproductive life may span 20 years and it has been known to live to the grand old age of 50, although this is extremely exceptional in the wild.

When hunting, the Siberian tiger has a good choice of prey, including Ussuri sika, Amur goral, musk deer (*Moschus moschiferus*) and even the Ussuri black bear. However, one of its favourite victims is the wild boar. These tenacious animals are widespread and can be found in many forests throughout the world, where they feed destructively, turning over large areas of soil in the search for succulent roots, bulbs and fungi. They are ideal prey for the tiger, weighing anything up to 750 lb (340 kg) in extreme cases and armed with only short, tusk-like teeth. Nonetheless the tiger must approach with caution, because the boars will struggle violently and can inflict nasty wounds. The tiger's tactics with all large prey are the same: on first sight or scent it commences stalking, making a slow, stealthy progress towards its intended victim. When 10–30 yards (3–9 m) from its prey it springs into the attack, crashing down on the animal's back and biting into its neck, often severing the jugular and crushing the spine with its fangs. It then drags its prey to any nearby secluded place where it can devour more than 100 lb (45 kg) in one sitting.

The tiger may stay with a large carcass for ten days but occasionally wanders off, at which time wolves, black bears, foxes (*Vulpes vulpes*) and even nutcrackers quickly take advantage of its absence to scavenge what they can. There are even reports of brown bears trailing tigers, probably in the hope of just such a free feed.

Outside the nature reserves man is a fierce competitor of the tiger for the wild boar, but fortunately the boars are capable of prodigous feats of reproduction and can double or triple their numbers in one year if they are not hunted by man or beast.

The tiger's hunting range takes it from the river valleys up to the peaks of the Sikhote Alin. In these heights the rare Amur goral (*Naemorhedus caudatus*) lives in small herds, feeding on acorns and leaves. The goral is usually described as a goat-antelope, with a broad chest, donkey-like ears, and short horns which it keeps deadly sharp by rubbing them against rocks and trees. It is well camouflaged, its grey coat blending into the rocky screes to which it keeps in an attempt to avoid tigers and wolves. There are now only about 300 Amur goral left in the Sikhote Alin range and as such they

The Siberian tiger, the largest tiger in the world; its colouring is generally lighter than that of other tigers, with large patches of white on the chest and underbelly. Its fur grows longer in the winter, helping it withstand the low temperatures.

are no longer a major prey for the tigers, although in the Lazovsky reserve for one they are still relentlessly pursued. The goral is now protected from the human hunting that reduced it to its current rare status.

Another prey of the Siberian tiger that is becoming increasingly rare is the musk deer. This tiny deer stands less than 2 ft (60 cm) high at the shoulder and, without horns, can defend itself only with the tusk-like canines that protrude from its upper lip. These animals often fall prey to the tiger in the central area of the Sikhote Alin, where they are relatively numerous. For centuries they have been hunted for the musk secreted by a small abdominal gland, which is used in perfumes and especially valued by the Chinese for its dubious properties as an aphrodisiac.

The Ussuri black bear is also sometimes the tiger's victim, particularly in winter when the tiger locates a den. Earlier this century L. G. Kaplanov, a Russian naturalist who spent a month trailing a tiger on foot and on skis, heroically living off the remains of its kills in sub-zero temperatures, observed one such incident and described it in vivid detail. The tigress stalked towards the small den, digging a hole at the opposite side to the narrow entrance. She then pounced from one hole to the other, until with one great swipe of her paw she had caught the terrified bear by its foreleg, enabling her to drag it out of its winter retreat and despatch it in the usual manner.

Sika deer feeding on a farm in the Sikhote Alin Reserve. In the wild sika deer form part of the prey of the Siberian tiger.

OPPOSITE *A Siberian tiger cub, an example of the great success of the nature reserves which have raised the Siberian tiger population dramatically from the brink of extinction.*

The tiny musk deer is becoming increasingly rare. It is hunted for its musk, a wax-like secretion produced by a small gland on the abdomen of the male deer.

It is this flexibility in the selection of its prey that has allowed this super-predator to become re-established, but its numbers are now sufficiently high that in some areas it preys on livestock, pets and occasionally even man. This has led to a certain lack of popularity with some of the region's residents, especially those whose favourite pet dogs have disappeared down the throat of this great carnivore. Attacks on livestock are an inevitable consequence of man's encroachment on its habitat and food supply but, much as they enrage local farmers, they do not provoke the same strength of feeling as an attack on a human.

For more than 50 years there were no unprovoked attacks recorded until in 1976 a tractor driver was found partly eaten. Since then there has been a growing number of reports of maulings and tigers have been sighted wandering into the outskirts of Vladivostok, very suitably, in a way, for the official symbol of the city is the Siberian tiger. In the last three years four tigers have been recorded in the suburbs of the city. All were hunted down and killed. In Khabarovsk, further north, an old woman found a large tiger asleep in her hall. Terrified, she introduced her unfortunate pet cat to it in the hope that they would recognize each other as distant relatives, but the cat made an exceptionally fast exit without disturbing the tiger in the least. The story had a happy ending, though, for the lady's husband locked it in

Once hunted, the elegant goitred gazelle is now protected in a number of reserves in Russia. Wolves are the gazelle's main predator during the winter months.

the hall until it could be anaesthetized and transported safely to a reserve.

The continued conservation of the Siberian tiger will need careful management as the region's population rises and the loss of habitat continues. As it is, the territory in the nature reserves, large as it may be, is not large enough for a higher tiger population, and various measures are being put forward, including a ban on hunting certain prey species and an increase in the size of some reserves such as the Sikhote Alin. A Soviet–American programme is under way to radio-tag tigers in order to understand them better. There has been much debate on how to cope with the tiger's increasing encroachment on settlements, and suggestions have ranged from capturing cubs for zoos to organizing selective hunting for foreign 'sportsmen' able to pay an extremely high price.

However, there are now more than 600 Siberian tigers in captivity, far more than in the wild, and it is doubtful whether more are necessary (or wanted by zoos) to maintain a genetically viable breeding pool. It would be useful to interbreed some of the wild stock with the captive population, both in captivity and in the wild, by using such techniques as artificial insemination. Since the wild population comes from only 20–30 'ancestors', such 'gene mixing' would increase the genetic diversity and fitness of the wild population, reducing the risks of inbreeding.

There is surely a case for the conservation of far more of this region, so rich is its diversity of flora and fauna. Yet a 30-year contract has recently been concluded – without any assessment of the environmental impact – between a Soviet corporation, Primorsklesprom (Maritime Region Forestry Industry), and the giant South Korean firm Hyundai, for logging forests north of the Sikhote Alin reserve. In the first five-year period 1.05 million cubic yards (800,000 cu m) of timber will be clear-felled, which will totally denude the upper part of the Peya river basin. Reafforestation is planned to protect against erosion but will not afford protection for the first 20 years.

Scientists at the Academy of Sciences' Far Eastern Centre in Vladivostok are extremely concerned about the likely consequences, for large-scale clear-felling will inevitably result in the run-off of snowmelt and rain carrying resinous pollutants and some of the annual 163,500 cubic yards (125,000 cu m) of waste into the rivers. This will seriously threaten fish stocks and the whole web of life dependent on them. But what makes the matter worse is that the Bikin river into which the area's smaller rivers flow is an area of magnificent forest in its primary, virgin state with one of the greatest concentrations of both sables and tigers and the chief breeding area for the endemic scaly-sided merganser (*Mergus squamatus*), one of the world's rarest wildfowl. The scaly-sided merganser would be one of the first species to be affected as it is dependent on the fish of the Bikin river for its food source. Serious pollution could push it to the edge of extinction.

With hundreds of forestry workers brought into the area to live, new settlements, roads, a projected new port on the coast and the general disturbance of the forest, the Nanai and Udegey peoples' fishing and trapping lives are being threatened and their traditional skills lost as the younger generation is tempted by the wages of the forestry industry.

The project has gone ahead at such speed that locals believe the intention is to make it impossible to stop if opposition grows. The whole story is indeed an epitome of the sort of dilemma which will increasingly face the authorities in the now disintegrated Soviet Union. In a desperate economic situation with foreign currency urgently needed, are they to turn their backs on such huge deals? Surely the answer is that all factors, including the environmental and sociological ones, must be taken into account – in public – and that only then should decisions be made. That may now be possible in the new society which is now emerging.

With the huge changes taking place, what lies ahead for the future of Russia and its wildlife? The massive environmental problems have reached a critical state and both the human and wildlife populations suffer. Funding will be in short supply with so many other priorities but international aid and collaboration should soon start to improve the situation. The rapid growth of an active – and activist – green movement has already proved effective, and both education and the media are continually increasing the environmental awareness which began so much later than in the West. Another positive factor will be the shift of initiative and responsibility from the state to the individual.

In the words of Chekhov's most famous play, *The Cherry Orchard*, 'Lord, you've given us vast forests, boundless fields, far-flung horizons and since we live here, we ought to be real giants ourselves.'

A female mink emerging from winter hibernation.

Michael Pitts, cameraman in Sikhote Alin, the Soviet Far East

Flying across Russia from Moscow to Vladivostok, we passed over the Russian steppes, the Ural mountains, Lake Baikal and great expanses of forest wilderness. Next we boarded an old single-engined Antonov biplane and flew north to our destination – the small coastal fishing village of Ternai. Below us lay a seemingly endless forest of cedar, silver birch and Manchurian oaks, all lightly dusted in a fine coat of snow.

Our assignment was to film the Siberian tiger and our chances of success were to depend greatly on our woodsman and tracker, Viktor. We left Ternai quickly; spring was approaching and already patches of ground were appearing through the snow. Tracking a fully grown tiger in thick snow was relatively easy, but across hard ground and rock our task would be much more difficult.

As we drove south towards Lake Blagadatney we came to deep snow-filled gullies and ravines as we went deeper into the forest. We reached a large clearing where our hut stood on a small hill. To the south lay the lake, completely frozen over. Beyond it lay heavily forested hills and to the west rose the imposing snow-covered peak of Mount Sikhote, tallest in the Sikhote Alin range. To the east lay the slate-blue waters of the Pacific Ocean, the sea's surface flecked with foam whipped up by the unrelenting icy wind, which carried the scent of pines and sea air.

Our search for the tiger was to start here as its prey of sika deer and wild boar would migrate to the coast at this time of year. Near the sea the snow was less deep and food easier to find. The deer sometimes make their way to the seashore to feed on seaweed thrown up by the heavy surf.

The following morning we set off into the dense forest which quickly enveloped us. Within an hour we saw the carcass of a fully grown male boar which had clearly been the victim of a tiger attack. Although wounded it had escaped and died here rather than becoming food for its assailant which, given the size of the boar's tusks, could have been injured itself in the attack. Nearing a rise in the forest, Viktor suddenly raised his hand for silence. We had inadvertently come upon a herd of wild boar digging in the snow uncovering dead leaves and roots. They quickly caught our scent and bolted off into the trees, squealing as they went.

Early in the afternoon we reached the seashore and turned north to follow the coast for a short distance before going back into the forest. There was little snow here but the sand particles thrown up by the wind were like a thousand needles on the skin. Walking with my head down, I stumbled onto the carcass of a sika deer, obviously caught by a tiger. Like the boar we had found earlier, it had been dead for some time so there were no tracks for us to follow.

By mid-afternoon we were climbing toward the crest of a ridge of hills. Suddenly Viktor dropped to one knee and told us to hurry. As I drew near I picked out the tracks of a large animal – the paw marks of a tiger fresh from the previous evening, running parallel to the path we were on. The tracks disappeared on hard ground and re-emerged in the patches of snow. Every so often Viktor would stop to pull tiger hairs from the bark of trees on which it had rubbed itself. The tracks eventually veered off the trail we were following and had headed inland. We were so close yet so far; it was impossible to continue that day as the light was fading but I looked after the tracks into the darkening forest before turning towards the lights of our hut upon the hill.

PICTURE CREDITS

The publishers and author would like to thank Survival Anglia and the following photographers for use of their pictures:

title page Konrad Wöhte
contents page Konrad Wöhte

9 Chris Catton
11 Richard Kemp
13 Konrad Wöhte
14 Chris Catton
15 Barbara Maas
17 Richard Kemp
18 Bomford and Borrill
20 (upper) Chris Catton
   (lower) Michael Day
21 Rick Price
22 Richard Kemp
25 Konrad Wöhte
26 Arvidas Baronas
29 Richard Kemp and Piers Finzel
31 Andrey Zvoznikov
32 Richard Kemp
35 Richard Kemp and Piers Finzel
36 Richard Kemp
38 Michael Day
39 Michael Day
40 Andrey Zvoznikov
42 Richard Kemp
43 Andrey Zvoznikov
44 Richard Kemp
45 Richard Kemp
47 Joel Bennett
53 David Shale
55 Konrad Wöhte
57 Konrad Wöhte
58 Konrad Wöhte
60 Bomford and Borkowski
61 Konrad Wöhte
63 Michael Day
64 Jeff Foott
66 Konrad Wöhte
67 Michel Strobino
68 Joe B Blossom
70 Liz and Tony Bomford
72 Konrad Wöhte
73 Konrad Wöhte
75 Konrad Wöhte
76 Konrad Wöhte
79 Konrad Wöhte
81 Rick Price
82 Joe B Blossom
85 Bomford and Borrill
88 Liz and Tony Bomford
90 John Bulmer
91 Konrad Wöhte
92 Joe B Blossom

95 Bomford and Borkowski
99 John Bulmer
101 John Bulmer
103 Chris Catton
106 Chris Catton
110 Herbert Kogler
113 Chris Catton
114 Chris Catton
117 Jeff Foott
118 Michael Day
119 Chris Catton
121 Bomford and Borrill
123 Bomford and Borrill
124 Andrey Zvoznikov
127 Bomford and Borrill
128 Tony Bomford
129 Bomford and Borrill
131 Bomford and Borrill
132 Bomford and Borrill
134 Tony Bomford
136 Bomford and Borrill
137 Bomford and Borrill
138 Bomford and Borrill
139 Bomford and Borrill
141 Bomford and Borrill
143 Bomford and Borrill
144 Bomford and Borrill
147 Tony Bomford
149 Chris Catton
151 Chris Catton
152 Joel Bennett
155 Chris Catton
156 Tony Bomford
158 Rick Price
160 Jeff Foott
163 Jeff Foott
165 Rick Price
167 Michael Pitts
169 Michael Pitts
170 Michael Pitts
171 Michael Pitts
173 Joel Bennett
174 Richard Kemp
177 Michael Day
178 Michael Day
179 Michael Pitts
180 Vivek Sinha
181 Rick Price
182 Michael Pitts
184 Michael Pitts

BIBLIOGRAPHY

Allen, W. E.D., *A History of the Georgian People*, 1932. Reissued by Routledge & Kegan Paul, 1971

Appleby, John, *A Selective Index to Siberian, Far Eastern and Central Asian Russian Materia Medica*, Wellcome Unit for the History of Medicine, 1987

Armstrong, Terence et al, *The Circumpolar North*, Methuen, 1978

Baedeker's *Russia*, 1914, George Allen & Unwin, David & Charles, 1971

Baird, P. D., *The Polar World*, Longman, 1964

Bell, John, *A Journey from St Petersburg to Pekin, 1719–22*, (Stevenson, J. L., Ed., 1965), Edinburgh University Press, 1965

Berg, L. S., *Freshwater Fishes of the USSR and Adjacent Countries*, Israel Program for Scientific Translations, Jerusalem, 3 vols, 1962–1965.

Bibikov, D. I., Zhirnov, L. V., et al, *Wolf in the USSR: Status & Management*, IUCN Wolf Group paper, Trondheim, 1988

Billington, J. H., *The Icon and the Axe*, Weidenfeld and Nicolson, 1966

Blanch, Lesley, *The Sabres of Paradise*, John Murray, 1960

Blum, Jerome, *Lord and Peasant in Russia*, Princeton University Press, 1972

Bobrinsky, N. A. et al, *Opredelitel' mlekopitayushchikh SSSR (A Guide to the Mammals of the USSR)*, Prosveshchenie, Moscow, 1965

Borodin, A. M., Gen. Ed., *Krasnaya Kniga SSSR (Red Data Book of the USSR)*, Vol. 1 (fauna), Lesnaya Promyshlennost', Moscow, 2nd edn. 1984

Brown, Archie, Ed. et al, *The Cambridge Encyclopaedia of Russia and the Soviet Union*, CUP, 1982

Carp, Erik, Compiler, *Directory of Wetlands of International Importance in the Western Palearctic*, IUCN-UNEP, 1980

Chernov, Yu, I., *The Living Tunda*, CUP, 1985

Clark, Tessa, (Ed.), *The Russian Chronicles*, Century, 1990.

Conolly, Violet, *Beyond the Urals*, OUP, 1967

Conquest, Robert, *The Harvest of Sorrow*, Arrow, 1988

Cramp, Stanley, (Ed.), *Handbook of Birds of Europe, Middle East, and North Africa*, 5 Vols, OUP for RSPB, 1988

Davydova, M., Koshevoi, V., *Nature Reserves in the USSR*, Progress, Moscow, 1989

Delacourt, Jean, *The Waterfowl of the World*, 4 vols. Country Life, London, 1954–64

Dement'ev, G. P. & Gladkov, M. A., *Birds of the USSR*, IPST, Jerusalem, 1966–68

Dmitryshn, Basil, (Ed.), *Medieval Russia: A Source Book, 900–1700*, The Dryden Press, Hinsdale, Illinois, 2nd Edn. 1973

Durrell, Gerald, *Durrell in Russia*, Guild Publishing, 1986

Flint, V. E. et al, *Field Guide to Birds of the USSR*, Princeton University Press, 1989

Gilbert, Martin, *Imperial Russian History Atlas*, Routledge and Kegan Paul, 1978

Gregory, J. S., *Russian Land, Soviet People*, Harrap, 1968

Groves, Colin P., *Horses, Asses & Zebras in the Wild*, David & Charles, 1974

Heiss, L., *Askania Nova: Animal Paradise in Russia*, Bodley Head, 1970

Herbert, Agnes, *Casuals in the Caucasus*, John Lane, The Bodley Head, 1912

Holcik, Juraj, (Ed.), *Freshwater Fishes of Europe*, Aula-Verlag, 1989

Hooson, David J. M., *The Soviet Union*, (A Systematic Regional Geography, Vol. 7), University of London Press, 1966

Howe, G. Melvyn, *The Soviet Union: A Geographical Study*, Macdonald and Evans, 1983

Hudson, Robert, *Threatened Birds of Europe*, Macmillan, 1975

Humphrey, Caroline, (Volume Ed.), *Peoples of the Earth*, Vol. 14, *East of the Urals*, The Danbury Press, 1973

IUCN East European Programme: *Environmental Status Reports: 1990. Vol 3: USSR.* IUCN, Cambridge, 1991

Jackson, W. A. Douglas, (Ed.), *Soviet Resource Management and the Environment*, 1978

Jorré, George, *The Soviet Union, the Land, and its People*, Longmans, 1963

Kerner, Robert, *The Urge to the Sea*, University of California Press, 1942

Knystautas, Algirdas, *The Natural History of the USSR*, Century, 1987

Kohl, J. G., *Russia*, 1842

Kolosov, A. M., Gen. Ed., *Krasnaya Kniga RSFSR* (Red Data Book of the RSFSR), Rossel' khozizdat, Moscow, 1983

Komarov, Boris, *The Destruction of Nature in the Soviet Union*, Pluto Press, 1979

Kochan, Lionel, et al., *The Making of Modern Russia*, Pelican, 1983

Kourennoff, Paul M. & St. George, George, *Russian Folk Medicine*, W. H. Allen, 1970

Levin, M. G. & Potapov, L. P., *The Peoples of Siberia*, University of Chicago, 1964

Macdonald, David, *Encyclopaedia of Mammals*, 2 vols, Allen & Unwin, 1984

Martin, Janet, *Treasure of the Land of Darkness*, CUP, 1986

Massey Stewart, John, (Ed.), *Lake Baikal: on the brink?*, Environmental Research Series, No. 2, IUCN East European Programme, 1991

Norman, Henry, *All the Russias*, William Heinemann, 1902

Nowak, Ronald M. & Paradiso, John L., *Walker's Mammals of the World*, Johns Hopkins University Press, Baltimore & London, 2 vols, 1983

Ognev, S. I., *Mammals of Eastern Europe & Northern Asia: (Mammals of the USSR and Adjacent Countries)*, 9 vols, IPST, Jerusalem, 1962–67

Pryde, Philip, *Conservation in the Soviet Union*, CUP, 1972

Pryde, Philip, *Environmental Management in the Soviet Union*, CUP, 1991

Red Data Book Series, IUCN

Rzoska, J. & Luther, H., *Project Aqua: A Source Book of Inland Waters Proposed for Conservation*, IBP Handbook No. 21, IUCN Occasional Paper, No. 2, IBP, Blackwell, 1971

Sokolov, V. E., Syroechkovsky, E. E. (Gen. Eds), *Zapovedniki SSSR (Nature Reserves of the USSR)*, 11 Vols., Mysl', Moscow 1985–

Stanek, V. J., *The Pictorial Encyclopedia of the Animal Kingdom*, Hamlyn, 1976

Stewart Hugh, *Provincial Russia*, A. & C. Black, 1913

Stroganov, S., *Carnivorous Mammals of Siberia*, IPST, Jerusalem, 1969

Suslov, S. P., *Physical Geography of Asiatic Russia*, W. H. Freeman, 1961

Syroechkovsky, S., *Wild Reindeer of the Soviet Union*, Amerind, New Delhi, 1984

Taaffe, Robert N. and Kingsbury, Robert C., *An Atlas of Soviet Affairs*, Methuen, 1965

Tochenov, V. V., *Atlas SSSR*, Moscow, 1987

Tooke, William, *View of the Russian Empire . . .*, 3 vols., 1799

Uspensky, S. M., *Life in High Latitudes: A Study of Bird Life*, Amerind, New Delhi, 1984

Utechin, S. V., *Everyman's Concise Encyclopaedia of Russia*, Dent, 1961

Vernadsky, George, *Kievan Russia*, Yale University Press, 1973

Vevers, G. M., *Animals of the USSR*, Heinemann, 1948

Zhadin, V. I. & Gerd, S. V., *Fauna and Flora of the Rivers, Lakes and Reservoirs of the USSR*, IPST, Jerusalem, 1963

Zhirnov, L. V., et al, *Redkie i izchezayushchie zhivotnye SSSR: mlekopitayushchie i ptitsy (Rare and disappearing fauna of the USSR: mammals and birds)*, Lesnaya promyshlennost', Moscow, 1978

Journals consulted include:

BBC Wildlife; *Current Digest of the Soviet Press*; *The Ecologist*; *Environmental Policy Review*: *The Soviet Union & Eastern Europe*; *Geographical Magazine*; *Journal of Icthyology*; *Marwell Zoo Papers*; *Moscow News*; *National Geographic Magazine*; *Natural History*; *Polar Record*; *Priroda* (in Russian); *New Scientist*; *Oryx* (Journal of the Flora & Fauna Preservation Society); *Science in the USSR*; *Soviet Union*; *Soviet Weekly*; *Sputnik*.

INDEX

ARCTIC

NOVAYA ZEMLYA

8

KOLA
PEN.

LAKE
LADOGA

St Petersburg

Novgorod • *Neva*

LAKE
ONEGA

WHITE
SEA

YAMAL PEN.

Pechora

Vorkuta •

VALDAI
HILLS

Moskva

Kiev •

MOSCOW •

12

S

U
R
A
L

M
T
S

Dnieper

Yeniseï

5

Volga

1

Irtysh

6

4

Ob

14

B
L
A
C
K

S
E
A

C
A
U
C
A
S
U
S

7

11

Novosibirsk •

Tbilisi •

C
A
S
P
I
A
N

S
E
A

*ARAL
SEA*

3

Syr Darya

Amu Darya

TIEN
SHAN

| 0 | | 800 Km |

| 0 | | 500 Miles |

PAMIRS

Map drawn by Raymond Turvey